Wen...

Beauty from Ashes

As told by Sharon Throop

With comments by Rev. Al Stewart, D.D.

PoBoy Publishing © 2020

All quotations and notes are mentioned with the source
right at the time of usage so there is no need for a
bibliography.

Special thanks to my dear friend Jessie Stewart of Liberty
University who did a painstakingly outstanding job in the
editing of this manuscript.

Take note that Chapters or comments by Rev. Al Stewart
will start with *(Words from Rev. Al)*

Table of Contents

Foreword

This book is so very powerful in many ways. As a suicide attempt survivor twice, I can personally relate to Wendy's story. Everyone's story is different, as we are all unique, however that low point that suicide victims, and survivors, find themselves in, is a common ground. It is a very dark place of desperation and hopelessness. Being a survivor, I can say this with total confidence...the individual struggling has lost all hope and feels that there is no way out of the pain except to end their life. Rational and clear thoughts do not exist in those last moments. And, as in Wendy's case, even those with a strong support system still believe that they can no longer hold on.

I can't speak for the exact thoughts and emotions in every suicide victim or survivor's case, however I can tell you this...sometimes it doesn't matter how many family members and friends that love and care about you, you just want out. You are ready to go. I say these things to shed some light on the mindset of someone struggling that severely, for those who cannot relate. And also to hopefully relieve any guilt that family or friends feel, such as wondering if there was more they could have done or said. Believe me when I say this, because I have been there more times that I can count...there is most likely nothing more you could have done or said.

At that point your loved one has made up their mind. I pray that friends and family left behind will know and believe this. With that said, please do not ever give up trying to reach your loved one, because yes, it can make a difference. I have a BA in Psychology and have worked in the mental health field for over 15 years. Because of my own personal struggle with depression for almost 30 years, my desire to help others struggling was the reason I chose the field I did. It has been challenging and even emotionally exhausting sometimes, but it has been more than worth it. I am a firm believer that our pain is never in vain. God wants to use our struggles to help others in the same life situations. And for that, our struggles and traumas are used for good, always. I was so incredibly inspired by Wendy's mother's courage, bravery, and strength in telling Wendy's, and her own, story. Her vulnerability moved me and warmed my heart so deeply. I cannot imagine the pain and sorrow she experienced, and the void that will be there until she is reunited with her beautiful daughter.

Sharon is a warrior in every sense of the word, and I hope and pray that this book will reach, and touch, every single person that reads it. I felt every emotion she was describing, because she was so courageously honest and raw. Hearing her personal story of the aftermath really spoke to me in the sense of how those left behind feel, and what their own dark place is like.

I hope that alone will give anyone contemplating suicide another perspective, that a mother and father's pain will give them the strength to hold on and to seek help. This is such a bittersweet, but beautiful, story. I am blessed to have been given the chance to read it. Lastly, Pastor Al did a beautiful job of writing the story of this precious girl and her family. He is such a faithful and caring pastor, and true friend to all who know him. He has a strong passion

5

to reach out to those in the low valleys and pull them back up. I pray Wendy's story, as told by Sharon, will lift up those in the valley right now. Praise God for salvation, and that we will one day be with our lost loved ones again.

-- Brandie Hanks, B.A.,Psychology,
Randolph Macon Women's College
(Now Randolph College)
Lynchburg, VA

Introduction

(Words from Rev. Al)

I have been encouraging Sharon to write this book for many years now. Needless to say on my recent trip to Geneva Ohio this past summer I was overjoyed when she finally agreed to consider such an endeavor. Let's face it, even those of us who have never experienced the loss of a child know enough that the lifelong effects of such a loss must be excruciating and unbelievably painful to say the least. Sadly losing a child is something that so many never get over and they find it difficult to carry on productively for the rest of their lives. After all, a part of them is now missing and this had certainly been the case here with Sharon as well as Bill, Wendy's stepdad who went home to be with the Lord in 2018.

Wendy's mom Sharon is truly one of the best and bravest people I have ever met. And I'm glad to say that in this case, there is a happier ending then most and you will read about it here! How a *"divine appointment"* from heaven brought a dramatic change to the Throop household way back in the early 2000's. An appointment I was most fortunate to be a part of. God really did bring *"beauty out of ashes"* and we'll talk more about that. Our journey together started about 3 years after Sharon's daughter Wendy took her life in 1996. I just happened by *"circumstance"* to come across her daughter's memorial page one night and found myself crying uncontrollably for quite some time. I had been focusing on ministry to parents whom had lost children to suicide at the time. Upon composing myself, I did what I thought any good Christian would do, I fired off a few emails of encouragement to Sharon and said what I thought were all the right things. Well, it didn't take long to get back a few rather unedited, raw, and honest to the bone replies from her. The thing I am most thankful for is that regardless of how *"raw"* her replies were, one thing was clear, they were unedited and honest! In looking back, I'm quite certain most Christians would have given up or moved on to someone else, but that began our story, friends. It is heart wrenching, it is going to be honest, it will have you smiling later in the book because of God's intervention, but also crying as I was when I read Wendy's story for the first time online. What is so unusual from my perspective about *"our story"* is that a young lady I've never met has been responsible for truly changing the course of my life, for changing my heart and emotions, and for bringing out the best in me, yet, it is someone I've never met! How unusual that must sound to so many of you, but it is true.

You will also find out that suicide never was nor is it as many have portrayed, even fellow Christians, a **"black and white or open and shut"** issue. I am grieved especially as a Pastor at how some fellow Pastors and Christian leaders have treated this topic by saying some unbiblical things. I am convinced that suicide must be handled on a *"case by case"* basis and here is why. Think about it, friends, we have no problem recognizing that people have diseases which cause them at times to act irrationally to be irritated or even irate at times causing instability. Add to that any legitimate chemical imbalances happening within that person and maybe most importantly, traumatic events that have taken place to the person involved whom due to this imbalance or disease may have little or no coping mechanism to deal with these things and then it's much easier to see how such a person can be pushed over the edge. And let us not forget another crucial factor, the spiritual factor. In the Gospel of John Jesus told us something important about Satan, the enemy of God and all mankind, In John 10:10 we read, "A thief (Satan) comes only to steal and kill and destroy". It should be obvious to all by looking around at this world before us that the enemy has done a brilliant job of causing death, and premature death. He is good at what he does, and he is there to help push a person to the point of going over the cliff. After all he's been doing it for well over 6,000 years now. The scripture also tells us that he prowls about the earth actively looking to destroy and devour the souls of men and women. 1 Peter 5:8 "Be sober-minded, be alert. Your adversary the devil is prowling around like a roaring lion, looking for anyone he can devour".

Having said that let me also share with you the good news. Going back to John and verse 10, I'm so thankful that the verse doesn't stop there. That very same verse finishes with these words of Jesus; "I have come so that they may have life and have it in abundance." So as you read the events that unfolded in Wendy's life, you will come to understand why I **now** believe this topic must be handled on a case by case basis. I know I speak for Sharon when I say that our prayer is that if just **one** person decides to choose life after reading this book, it is **all** worth the toil and the reopening of deep raw emotions and scars that went into the formation of this book. *(Trust me when I tell you there were a few times we had to stop and I frankly thought Sharon wouldn't be able to do it, but her courageous spirit, guided by our Heavenly Father, broke through, I'm so proud of her, friends!)*

As you will hear from Sharon, especially at the end of this book, reaching others who are struggling with mental health issues is the **only** reason why she agreed to tell her story and allow me to put it into print. Please allow me to say something here about a very special man, Wendy's stepdad, William *"Bill"* Throop. Bill passed away in 2018 and I had the great honor of presiding over his service in Ohio. Bill loved Wendy as though she was his own daughter. If you knew him, you'd know what I mean. Bill also carried a profound sense of guilt and grief because his gun case was not locked the day of the incident. I'm ever so thankful for the many intimate conversations we had together about those feelings he had and I was privileged to have a front row seat in seeing how the Lord Jesus Christ with a wave of His holy hand swept away those feelings from Bill's life. It was Bill who was responsible for what beauty came out of the ashes after losing a child. It was Bill who bought Sharon a computer so she could talk to others who shared their unexpected life change. It was also Bill who began to read my replies with interest and who would tell Sharon, *"this guy's right"*………
All of this culminated the next spring in me leaving my office one Friday morning and driving exactly 451 miles from Wolcott Ct. to Geneva Ohio to meet Bill and Sharon

just 3.5 years after Wendy's passing. Lastly, I want to say something for the benefit of those reading who have friends who have lost a child in any manner, but especially to suicide. Sadly, something appears after such a circumstance, and it is known as *"the elephant in the room"*. Suddenly, friends, even close friends begin to tail or fall off and now the family is not only left with dealing with an impossible loss, but as an added hurt, the loss of close friends as well. May I ask you to please listen closely if you are a friend of someone like Sharon who has suffered a tremendous loss? Don't abandon those friends because you don't know what to say or because it now feels awkward as they **need** you, perhaps now more than ever! As a Pastor, I often practice what I call *"the ministry of presence or silence"* when I find myself comforting a family in loss. Something I'm sad to say I've had to do many times. Just your presence there is often enough; trust me when I say that.

Be willing to stop by with no agenda whatsoever, just be there, listen and offer hugs when needed, but please do not abandon them. As I stated earlier, they need you even if they don't verbalize it. To this day I will never forget my friend who went home to be with the Lord a few years ago, Al Yale. My son upon our moving to a new apartment many years ago in the 80's, somehow followed a dog into the woods as there was a huge state forest behind our complex. It happened in a matter of minutes, suddenly he was gone and everyone was frantic. By the grace of God, although he ended up sleeping in the woods that night, he was found the next morning and was fine. Truth is my best recollection of that horrifying event is remembering how my friend Al never left us all night. A newspaper reporter came to our Apartment after my son was found to interview us from my hometown paper; The Waterbury Republican-American. The reporter concluded the article by saying *"next to the Stewart family was a close friend soundly asleep on the couch"*. Al was still there, and that's what I'm talking about, friends. Prepare to be challenged and for your emotions to come alive by a true story of *"Beauty from Ashes".* I am particularly happy that three mental health professionals, that I have known personally and have respected for many years took the time to endorse this book. I know it was also a real blessing to Sharon as well. Despite how difficult it was to *"revisit"* those places and feelings that had been in a sort of *"hibernation"* for years.

For the record, as an independent writer and publisher, it is quite hard to get the word out about my books. The cost can really be prohibitive. With that said, if after reading this book, you think it is a book that needs to get into the hands of those who are hurting from such a loss, or are struggling with mental health issues, please feel free to do whatever you can to help us promote it by leaving a positive review on the Amazon book page, that's important. May God bless you as you do!

Pastor Al Stewart,

7/22/19, 6:59 pm.

Chapter One
It's A Girl!

Wendy was born on a rainy Saturday morning; June 18, 1977, after our car broke down on the way to the hospital. We had to proceed there with the help of an ambulance. The staff was all waiting for me when I arrived.

Wendy, June 18th, 1977

As Wendy grew and became the wonderful person that she turned into, she also developed into a wonderful young lady and was fiercely loyal to all her friends and family.

Truth is, we all marveled at her attributes and while she may not have been the wisest or prettiest, in our world she certainly was all that and more! Wendy graduated from Geneva High School in 1995. She ranked 13th out of 221 people which was an awesome feat in my opinion and with that ranking she received grants and scholarships to attend Ohio Wesleyan University *(OWU)* down in Delaware which is located a little North of Columbus, Ohio. Me, I as the mom was heartbroken that she was going so far away, but I was also very proud of her accomplishments. The dreaded day finally arrived and she packed up to go off to college and we loaded the car, *(to the hilt).* She was excited, nervous, and seemed somewhat ambivalent about the whole affair due to it being the beginning of a new life of independence on her own.

Wendy at 7 years old

14

Wendy at Graduation with Owen

She had a really busy summer working and getting all her ducks in a row before the start of her college year in the fall. We even had a 1-800 number added to our phone so she could call home without worrying about phone bills on her end from college.

Owen, pictured above, was one of Wendy's best friends throughout school. He truly became a surrogate son to us and **especially** during the time after Wendy passed. He helped us see the tomorrow in our lives. He spent many of his days and nights with us to try and figure out what had transpired that day which caused this great loss for us all. In fact it was Owen who received the last email from Wendy on the day of her death just before she left school that morning simply telling him she was looking forward to spending time with him over the Thanksgiving break. And although he lives a couple of states away with his family we keep in touch and he shares his family with me whenever he visits back home and calls me often as well.

He is a very important part of my life and will remain so until my time here is completed.

College started and she tried very hard to fit in and to roll with all the punches of the classes studying and of course, all the partying that went along with it. In December of 1995 she attended a party at a frat house and although we don't know all the details, sadly she was date-raped there and it was truly the beginning of the end.....She told no one really and came home for Christmas break with so much weighing on her mind. The third week of being home she went to visit her dad and once again he was piling on some emotional issues and she came home very late that night. I was so angry when she finally got home, I just blew up at her and for the first time in a long time, I just went to bed and didn't even say goodnight. *(I will never forgive myself for my part in that day)* My husband, Bill, also went to bed without really talking to her about my outburst, etc. The poor girl was feeling so lost. She then proceeded to call a very good friend to unload some of the emotional baggage that had built up that day and the preceding weeks. She even told him about the rape. Not knowing what to say, he said mostly nothing. I guess that is when she snapped the first time and decided that we all would be better off without her here. She took my husband's anxiety pills and went to the bathroom with a knife from our kitchen and began to cut her wrist. Fortunately, my husband got up and after deciding that she was **not** taking a shower, found her before it was fatal...

After calling the emergency squad, we immediately went to the hospital where she got stitched up and was sent to a psychiatric unit for a week. It was at this time that Wendy confirmed the rape. I beat myself up to this day to think that I heaped so much more upon her in that period of her life. I surmised that something dire had occurred when a young man that she had been dating, and had also been a large topic of conversation with us for weeks, suddenly disappeared from her conversations.

She went through a roller coaster of emotions and per her wishes; I did not let her friends know what had transpired. I simply told the many number of people that called to talk to her that she was ill and unable to return their call at this present time, but I promised that she would call them back or email from school.

After a week the doctors pronounced her just overwhelmed and said that we had to respect her decisions. Well you know what? Her decision still gnaws at me, and she wanted to return to school against our wishes. However, as the doctor had suggested, we backed her decision.

This is where I wished that doctors would not only treat the patient at hand, but get outside family viewpoints and thoughts to make a more informed decision or prognosis. During the family doctor visits when Bill or I would bring something up that had happened she would try and shush us and sweep it under the rug. Apparently the doctors did not see that behavior as destructive toward her prognosis, and felt she should return to school and would be fine. However, she made it through the semester, but not in the way I would have hoped for. Her grades were not the best, but there was always time to deal with that later. She seemed to be dealing with her past experiences very well.

She was pledged from every sorority on the campus and decided that she wanted to go for it, so she became a Delta Delta Delta. She really seemed like she was becoming her old self again so I committed myself to the *"letting her fly on her own"* syndrome. Lord, were we wrong. Something that we now know can never be reversed.........

Wendy and friends from her Sorority

Letting her go was one of the hardest things we had done in our lives at that point, as we did not feel she was returning to school with enough support.

The doctor made sure she would have counselling when she returned, but it turned out she only went two times and did not continue. Because she was over 18, the counselor had no obligation to let us or the doctor know that she had opted out! This is something that should be looked into. I believe that when there is a crisis in someone's life, there should be safeguards in place to manage any subsequent issues that could arise. Further support should be made available if and when needed also. In short, some type of follow up should be made to be sure the person is following through and getting the help they need. The summer of 1996 came and she took two jobs. One job was on the weekends and some evenings bussing tables at a local 100 year old tavern/eatery, and the other at a factory that her dad was employed at. She had a grand plan to save enough money to go to the Bahamas to take an extra credit class in marine biology *(one great little vacation too!!)*. She did get the opportunity to go to Chicago to visit some of her classmates for 5 days which was her first, and what turned out unbeknownst to us, the only trip she made on her own. We were all very proud that she managed so well. However, after her trip, her car broke down *(she had a 93 Blue Ford Mustang, and boy, did she love that car!)* and the transmission had to be rebuilt. It was in the dealership for over 5 weeks as they fixed one thing in the transmission after another. In the meantime, she had an old *"rust bucket"* to drive around in, and was very short-tempered about the whole thing. We finally got the car back one week before she was to return to school. *(Sigh of relief)* We packed up all her gear in her car and ours, and proceeded to make the trip back down to Delaware, OH. She had a new dorm with no air conditioning. Wendy and her roommates referred to their living quarters as the *"boring dorm."* I guess they used to go out in the hall and scream, *"Quit studying!"*

This time, for the school year, I was so strong and certain about leaving her there on her own. I saw a bunch of parents with first year students, melting in their emotions. I knew Wendy was a different girl and was going to be one tough cookie. She had her plans and she was going to stick to them. There was one amazing thing I did see while I was there, maybe a premonition, who knows? It happened when I went outside to get a breath of fresh air. No one was around at the time and I saw what looked like a bunch of stars floating in weird patterns in the sky. I followed them with my eyes and they started to drift behind some trees, so I got up to continue to follow them in that strange pattern. Then, one by one, they just flew straight up in the sky and disappeared. *(It was a wonderful sunny day, not dark at all).* I looked around to get someone else's confirmation, but I was still there alone. Was this a warning or just heat-stroke? I don't really know, in fact I probably never will...

Wendy with her beloved cat, Bishop

By September she was in full swing with school. She called home frequently and even called me at work just to chat. It was like old times. She met a boy that she really liked and we were so glad that she could commit to someone above just a friendship. We thought the worst was truly behind her.

She came home for a weekend in October. It was great fun having her around. We didn't do anything extravagant just family stuff. We had cook outs, and sat around our fire pit outside, catching up on all that was going on with her life and ours. We went to the local fall time fair nearby and looked at all the pumpkins. In fact, I had gotten her a cute little pumpkin with flowers on it. I also sent some Indian corn back to the dorm with her. On our way home, she got very serious with me and asked if we were going to be all right. *(Financially, it was tough as we had to pay for most of her medical bills for the earlier attempt on her life)*.

We then made plans to go see her for the day on parent's weekend, a week later in October at her College. In the end, I told her all was fine. We had it all worked out and by her subsequent college years, we would be fine to finish helping her as we had all planned. I told her not to worry about it or to be worried about us.

Chapter Two
Storm Clouds Brewing

We saw Wendy one last time when we went to her College for parent's weekend in late October. She was extremely tired, having gone to a concert the night before in Pittsburgh. She was upset though because all the parades and other events had been cancelled, as they had a tragedy on the campus the week before. At one of the frat houses, a fire had broken out and one young man did not make it. Although she knew him by face, she told us that she did not really know him. We assured her that we understood and felt so badly for his family and friends. We decided to attend her sorority tea and meet with some of her professors and friends, which was a swell idea for us.

Being that she was so tired, we left in the afternoon after having lunch, we drove back home to Geneva. If we had only known that this would be the last time we would ever see her alive, we would have stayed forever. The curious thing was, she **never** watched us leave. She said it made her sad, but that day she watched us leave and waved. Was this a portent too?

We spoke on the phone a few times after that date, but the last conversation we had was on Election Day Nov. 5th, 1996. I was teasing her about voting, as I had tricked her earlier in the spring when I had prepared her income taxes. I had her sign a voter registration form, along with her income tax forms. She simply did not pay attention to what she was signing and that the voter registration form was included. She had told me that she did not want to be a voter at that time in her life because she did not pay enough attention to issues and candidates. She was too busy and could find no time for this type of important duty. She was quite amazed when she received the notification that she could vote and asked me how I got her signature. We had a chuckle over this, but she did not vote. She also seemed a bit tense and down on herself regarding her grades and her focus. She had chosen to change her major to education and was going to shift over to being a guidance counselor for education instead of Zoology. She was attending and aiding in a local elementary school a couple of times a week and said she was enjoying the children, and she seemed pleased with her change of major. We were happy that she had lessened her workload and we told her being in education was a good move.

We hoped that one day she would perhaps have a marriage and a family because it would fit nicely with that lifestyle. We tried to assure her with the old adages, *"Just do the best you can do".* We truly felt she would be fine. She always had the option of taking a break as the money was set aside for her College one way or the other. What fools we were. I asked her if she could come home for the weekend before Thanksgiving break. She said couldn't because she had so many reports, and sorority obligations. I told her that it was okay and we would talk to her again and she said, of course you will. But sadly that never happened, what she said wasn't true as that was the last time we spoke. It is very hard to look back on these events and not feel all the regret of allowing her to return to College there. I know that in my heart of hearts we should have optioned our rights as parents and not allowed her to return without the support that she needed. I wish we had made that a requirement. I miss her smile, laughter and easy going, sister-like quality that she and I shared. Bill would always say to us, *"How's Wendy and her sister?"*

I even miss her complaining and whining about anything and everything. Sadly, you cannot return to those days and second guess every little nuance. To do so will allow yourself to be eaten alive. And for quite some time it did just that.

Chapter Three
the Event

On November 11th, 1996, the snows started to come down in Northeastern Ohio. The snow did not quit for almost a week and I stayed home that day from work because the weather was so bad. I had a grand day. I cleaned, cooked a great dinner *(sometimes I think it was the last nice dinner I ever cooked),* baked, and finished a cross-stitch for my hubby and I's tenth anniversary that was coming up next month. The next day, although the snow had not let up, I still decided I should go to work. Bill however wanted me to stay home and I so I initially agreed; but in the end, we both went to work. My day went slow due to the weather so I decided I would leave around noon, but we had gotten a new computer. I stayed to help set it up and get it going. I didn't end up leaving until 4:00 pm and upon finally hitting the road, it was slow going at best and I didn't arrive home until around 4:30 or so. It was snowing so hard I opened the garage from the road to get a good look at how deep the snow was piling up, when to my amazement I saw a car in the garage where I would normally park. I finally made it through the snow and once inside the garage I saw that it was Wendy's car! Needless to say, I got excited and yet scared all at the same time. The why's started...*"Why didn't she call me, why was she home, why, why, why?"*

Upon entering the house all was quiet, in fact, too quiet. I was so worried that I didn't even remove my jacket as I kicked off my shoes. My 87 year old mom lived with us at that time. I found her reading and I asked her where Wendy was. She commented on what a nice surprise it was that she was home and said that she must be upstairs changing. I yelled for Wendy over and over and upon receiving no reply, I finally mounted the stairs. Once at the top of the stairs, I saw something all over the door which was wide open. Thinking she spilled something, I figured I would find her asleep from her long drive home. *(One of her favorite past-times)*

I did find her asleep, eternally, as I rounded the top of the stairs to her room. I still did not believe until I saw the rifle lying next to her...I fell down the stairs, all the while screaming. I immediately called my neighbor, instead of calling 911. I was in shock. It was my first instinct because our neighbors had always been our *"go- to"* people for many years.

My Neighbor within minutes came running over and his wife immediately called 911. When the EMT's arrived along with the fire department personnel, they told me if they had been standing right next to her that they still could **NOT** have saved her. They had all known Wendy for most of her life and were just as lost as we were. One of the EMT's told me as they ran through the house that they would save her again, but that was not to be.

We all waited for Bill to come home from work. The house was continuously full of rescue personnel, neighbors, detectives and sheriffs *(when someone dies by their own hand they still have to evaluate the scene for an outside crime).* All the while, my poor, dead daughter is lying on the floor upstairs in our house. I was desperately waiting for Bill to come home. It took him over 3 hours due to the horrible weather and the fact that he worked some overtime to help make up for the time I spent at home the day before.

Can you imagine coming down a rural road and seeing all the flashing lights, etc. at your house? I pleaded for the rescue personnel to please stay as I knew he would be devastated. Of course, when he finally made it home, he thought it was my mom *(who was 87 then)*. He said to himself *"why are there so many cars?"* Apparently, Bill never saw the coroner's car. He had to leave his truck on the side of the road and was rushing up the driveway in the driving snowstorm. I ran out to meet him to tell him what had happened. I had an extremely difficult time in telling him that Wendy had died and just cried and moaned that Wendy was gone. He told me *"no, she is at college".* I told him that her car was in the garage, and that she had come home around 1:00 pm or so. Our neighbor had seen her, but did not think anything of it at the time. We both wept and were broken beyond imagination.

After sometime passed, our fire/rescue personnel made sure that Bill was okay and that we had some support, only then did they leave. After a lengthy time, the detectives released the body and the coroner spoke to us before removing her from our house. He told us that it was the second suicide within a month that he had to preside over and that they would not release any information quickly to assure that no media would contact us and cause further distress. There were so many people calling, or coming over. I do not remember most of that first night. I just remember that I could not go upstairs again for a long while. The weeping and sobbing were palatable and without Bill, family and the support of friends, I would have surely followed Wendy.

After all, what do you do after you lose your child by their own hand? The shock is overwhelming and there is nothing anyone can say or do that helps. Bill and I clung to each other that first night, and, needless to say, we couldn't find any sleep whatsoever.

(Words from Rev. Al)

I want to interject something very important at this point. I am writing this specifically to anyone who feels that life is not worth living, but have taken the time to read this book. Although, by the time I met up with Bill and Sharon, Wendy had been gone for close to 4 years, it was still apparent to me that they were dealing with many *"aftershocks"* and trauma from losing their daughter. As you have just read and will continue to read in the next chapter, I believe this is a good place and time in the book for anyone struggling in this manner to consider the impact **your** loss would have on those around you. And I don't say that to try to lay any guilt on you my dear friend.

I say this, because I want you to see how much you are loved, yes, even if you don't feel or think that! The sense of despair I believe plays a great part in one feeling that they have little to no worth, but nothing could be further from the truth! Just look at how deeply Bill and Sharon grieved. It is because what a fellow minister who wrote a book about grief once told me is very true. *"Those who have loved much, grieve much".* Never were words spoken so true.

Wendy was deeply loved and so are you. Please know that, please consider that. The Author of the New Testament book of Hebrews tells us in chapter 13 and verse 5 that God has promised to *"never leave or forsake us".* And in verse 6 he states that *"the Lord is my helper".* In your worse times of suffering, like many of us who call ourselves Christians have, so can you call upon that name, the name that the Bible tells us is *"above every other name".* That is the name of Jesus Christ. God loves you and so do we my friend, life is always worth living.

Chapter Four
Aftermath

Why did she do this? I'm not sure we will ever know all the answers. She left no note and piecing the information together here's what we do know. Wendy left the school at around 8:30 am. She should have gone to class, but came home instead. They had been looking for her for hours, but they did not call us. However, they did call our home and leave a message on the machine, but the time stamp showed it was after she died when they finally tried to find us with the news that we should be on the lookout for her or that there might be an issue. Again this is something that should be addressed by all schools. If someone goes missing and it is deemed unusual, first priority should be to contact the family.

We figure that she arrived home somewhere around 1:00 pm, as my neighbor saw her come in. Then she made two phone calls back to the school around 1:30 pm and she died somewhere between 1:30 and 2:00 pm, according to the coroner. My beautiful, talented, and loving daughter left this world all alone and by her own hand. We went through all the stages of pain and it was incredibly difficult to bear. There was anger, hurt and just utter disbelief. *(I actually thought that she mailed us a letter or left us something somewhere or somehow, up until a number of days passed and nothing materialized).* Lastly, there is just plain numbness as each day that you awake, after you can sleep again, only to find that the nightmare is real and that what happened is your life now.

There is nothing in this world that is so bad that cannot be dealt with in some way, but one thing, and that is death. There is no fix for that. The loss stays with us forever in this life. However, as you will read, I have found out that peace can return! As the title of this book suggests as does God's Word, *"beauty can come from ashes"*. As Pastor Al mentioned in his introduction, if this long, heart wrenching story helps just **one person**, then make no doubt about it, I will have done something with this terrible tragedy to help another. For that I am deeply grateful and can find some solace and sense in my daughter's death. I am reminded of Jesus word's which Pastor Al shared with Bill and me upon meeting us many years ago. The words have helped me to gain some peace and perspective since the Lord Himself spoke of life coming out of death. This passage helped Al as well upon the death of a good friend, an event which ultimately lead him to Christ and in return helped him to lead us to Christ. Amazing indeed!

John 12:24 *"Truly I tell you, unless a grain of wheat falls to the ground and dies, it remains by itself. But if it dies, it produces much fruit"*. It goes without saying that I'd want my daughter back if that was possible, but knowing that *"new life"* has come from her death, including the new life Bill and I now have in Christ gives us great peace in knowing that *"what Satan meant for evil, God meant for the good"*, as Joseph told his brothers when he came in contact with them through *"divine intervention"* after they had sold him into slavery. My prayer is that Wendy's life

31

and death will be that *"grain of wheat"* for many yet to come through this book.

In looking back, even to when Wendy first passed from this life, I remembered an incident that happened at the grocery store just before her funeral. The fire department had given us free use of their facilities for fellowship and food after the service. So many friends helped with this function and provided food and refreshments. I had ordered a couple of sandwich trays from our local supermarket, as I felt the need to help out with this fellowship. I insisted that I go alone to pick them up with concern from my family and friends. When I arrived at the deli counter, the only person I saw was a fellow classmate from the high school that Wendy attended and graduated from in 1995. I really did not want to speak to her and just wanted to pick up the trays and leave. She seemed quite anxious herself, but there we were face to face.

Being the mom that I always tried to be I asked her how she was doing. She began to stumble over all her words and blurted out that she was so sorry to hear about Wendy and that she was planning on going to the funeral, but she had to work. I told her that was understandable and hoped that she had gotten the opportunity to speak to her family about the tragic events that had happened. She assured me that she had done just that. She helped me all the way out of the store and I was extremely grateful. When the funeral proceeded the next day, I was surprised to see that the young lady from the grocery store was there. She shook our hands on her way out, and I was glad to see that she attended after all. The next day after the funeral was finished and we walked across the street to go home. I could not bear the thought of getting into the limo to return to the funeral home, so we just walked.

The tears flowed freely and I finally found that terrible piece of our loss was complete, and we had finished what was expected of us at this time. The funeral director came to our home and told us that none of the students from college, *(two buses full)* the college administrators or other folks would leave until we made an appearance. I really was all done, but upon Bill's urging that we should honor Wendy's memory, we got our coats and went down to the fire station to get and give more hugs, thoughts and prayers!

We waded through the hundreds that attended and I was in the kitchen portion of the hall when the young lady from the store appeared. I gave her a hug and told her that I was really pleased that she was able to get off work and come, and that it had meant a great deal. She then began to tell me that she didn't want to come because she had been contemplating suicide. This young girl was afraid to see all the fallout from Wendy's death and the havoc and loss it had left. *(Remember Pastor Al's words at the end of the previous chapter here.)* I will be forever grateful for that day before the service when I went to the store alone and encountered this young woman! The truth be told was it not a divine appointment?

After Wendy's funeral was over, a short time later, the university held a memorial service in their Chapel. There were many there that came and shared stories, experiences and their memories of Wendy. We chose not to attend, as we were both wrung out with all the emotions of the past couple of weeks. The chaplain of the university had the service taped and brought it to us so we could watch it when we were ready. We included Owen in this event as he had become a huge part of our lives and he, like us, was also struggling with Wendy's loss.

I'd like to give a brief synopsis of what the Chaplain who did the service had to say. He began by telling how so many missed Wendy on this very large campus. He also talked about the fact that there were also many questions of how could this have happened. *(Bill & I were not the only ones caught completely off guard)* He also spoke about where Wendy was, in terms of the afterlife. He related the story to a little tree that held up so many in her world, but that she had had a terrible tragedy of personal assault that, along with a million little things, had prompted her to have deep, dark depression that she could not seem to climb out from under.

He went on to state that many had asked him where God was on that terrible day. *(Something I asked Pastor Al more than once when we began our discussions online over email)* The Chaplain explained that Jesus was right there when Wendy drove home for hours in a terrible snowstorm. God was right there when she climbed the stairs to locate the gun which ended her dark, painful depression. And He stepped aside, because He knew that

Wendy was in so much pain and turmoil. He wanted her pain to end and a new life to begin for her. There was not a dry eye in the auditorium where this memorial had taken place, as well as at our home when we played the VHS. Wendy may be gone from this flawed earthly world, but she will never be gone from the hearts and souls of those who loved her as we did.

Serious Food for Thought

When you lose someone in your family, particularly a child, especially to suicide, it places the survivors in a very vicarious state. You may isolate yourself and lock the world out. The first time you hear laughing or comedy, it becomes appalling that anyone or anything is funny. If your child, friend, or family member is contemplating such actions it is imperative that you reach out and let them know that you are there for them. It may not always be accepted, but praying and asking God for help with this endeavor is essential and should be done frequently. I honestly feel that if you find that your loved one is seriously depressed and you cannot seem to help them, ask a professional and get them the help that they need. They may be angry with you at the time but in the grand scheme of things it may save their life and your family. The complete loss of a part of your family creates huge chasms of pain that most marriages do not survive. Death seems to either bring you together or it drives you apart. Everyone grieves differently, and I know that without my spouse at that time and where I was at spiritually, I'm not sure I'd be living on this earth anymore. But Bill proved to be the exception and not the rule thank God. There was a point in time that I could not even get up to turn a light switch on that was only a few feet away. We are not supposed to be lost like this in such a fast-paced world. We had co-workers, neighbors, friends and family that helped us through so many days and nights of feeling lost. Putting one foot in front of the other is not so terrible when you can share what you are feeling with a multitude of people that genuinely care about you and what happens in your *"new normal life"*. I cannot thank them enough for all that they did for us both and how they have helped over the years to keep our daughter's life and name alive.

(Words from Rev. Al)

Friends, in reading this chapter, I'm sure at least some of you were perplexed or even challenged in your heart and spirit by the words of that Chaplain who conducted Wendy's service. I didn't want to let an opportunity go by to talk more about the mind of God pertaining to things like suicide. I'm certain some of you, if you have walked with the Lord for many years, may have questioned the following portion of his message we just read a few pages back. Please allow me to repeat his words here. He went on to state that so many had asked him where God was on that terrible day. *(Something Sharon asked me more than once when we began our discussions online)* He explained that Jesus was right there when Wendy drove home for hours in that terrible snowstorm. God was right there when she climbed the stairs to locate the gun used to end her dark, depression. And maybe the most controversial thing he said was that God had stepped aside, because He knew that Wendy was in so much pain and turmoil and He wanted her pain to end and a new life to begin for her. It

36

is easy to read this and think that he was saying maybe God was *"okay"* with what took place, but nothing could be further from the truth! God's *"stepping aside",* as it were didn't mean that He didn't care or couldn't stop it! What it does mean is that in order for us to fully grasp or understand these things, we need to look back at Genesis 3 and revisit the fall of mankind. The fall of mankind reminds us of the flawed world we live in. It reminds us that this is *"our world"*, not the one that God wanted initially, but allowed in order for His creation to be *"free moral agents."* God did not create robots, He granted us a freed will, and He gave us the ability to choose. However, there's a fly in the ointment and frankly it's been there since that fateful day when that horrid act of disobedience took place in the Garden of Eden. That event passed on an *"Adamic nature"* to all of Adam and Eve's descendant's right up to you and me today.

The good news, however, is that the initial paradise God wanted for us all, which is spoken of with such eloquence in Revelation 21, will come to pass in the future and may be closer than any of us think! Now while there are indeed times where God clearly intervenes, and trust me I could write 500 pages on how He has time and time again, there are those occasions like Wendy's where He does not. *(In the way we want or expect!)* God is Sovereign. Thus, have to accept and believe that in each of these hard to understand circumstances, God is at work. In fact, this book is a Testament to that, is it not? How I became involved with a family from Ohio that I never knew and became introduced posthumously to a young lady that God would use to change the course of my own life, and by doing so would help bring what the title of this book so beautifully states *"beauty out of ashes"* can only be the hand of God at work in the midst of an excruciatingly terrible situation to bring good from something so bad. Only God can do that friends! As a close parallel, I am reminded of the subject of divine healing, or simply put, *"why some people get healed and others don't?"*

As a Pastor for many years now, I have witnessed countless healing *"divine interventions"*. In fact, just about every doctor over the course of his practice can tell you about a case he can only explain as having put away in his *"Jesus file"*. This file contains things that doctors just can't explain with logic or human reason. In the end, friends, if God did whatever we wanted Him to do, then I submit that He wouldn't be God, but rather He'd be more like a Genie granting us everything we want every time. Faith is what we are offered to help us through and the New Testament book of Hebrews chapter 11, verse 1 tells us exactly what faith is. *"Now faith is the reality of what is hoped for, the proof of what is not seen".* In closing this chapter, allow me to put it this way. We only see things from our end, from our perspective. But there is another, and that is God's perspective and it's the most important!

I will never forget reading the account of a man, who, for many years ran away from the call of God on his life. It ended up costing him his family, marriage, children and everything else. After many years, he finally surrendered to the Lordship of Jesus Christ and was getting back on his feet. He had recently started a construction job. In fact, his relationship with his children was even starting to experience healing. One day on the job, a crane many stories up from him was carrying a 700 lb. tile into the building, but somehow it found its way free of the crane and fell quickly to where this man was standing. He was only wearing a hard hat for protection. As you can imagine, it wasn't a pretty scene, but what the writer said at this point is something I think all of us must seriously think about when tragedies like Wendy's strike. She wrote the following; *"Perhaps when our friend looked up when he heard the yelling of those closes to him at the site, he didn't see a 700 lb. tile falling toward him with no time to flee, maybe he saw what the Prophet Isaiah said happens at the time of our death, an Angel coming to get him to usher him into the presence of Almighty God?"* Remember friends, there is always two perspectives, God's and then ours.

In the Old Testament book, Deuteronomy, we are told this in chapter 29 and verse 29; *"The hidden things belong to the Lord"*. I'm okay accepting the fact that we live as looking in a mirror *"dimly,"* but one day we will be *"face to face"* and will know and fully understand everything as 1st Corinthians 13:12 states.

Chapter Five
2 Years, 9 Months And Beyond

Wendy, 1995 preparing for a formal dance

We are well past the shock, the rage, and the devastation stages that come with the beginnings of being a survivor. Two years and nine months. This is how long we are now learning to live and forge a new path, one that is very different than what we ever dreamed. What comes next? For us, *(and I don't mean to step on toes here, as we are all different in how we deal and live after such events in our lives)* we have tried to help others in similar situations to see that it is not hopeless and that there are ways to feel like you are useful again. As you can see, my husband

and I have sought after the Lord again as the truth is, He never left us, we just sort of turned from Him for a time. Where was God you say? God was right there with Wendy when she felt so desperate, and so alone, and so useless that she felt she had no other choice but to leave this living world. He was right there as she went through our room looking, and searching, for the means to end the desperate pain that she found herself in. I think He was there and I know that He cried. But, I know He was there. He has continued to be with us to try and pick up the pieces of our lives and become valuable again on some level.

I have learned so much about this insidious disease *(i.e. depression, Yes it is a disease and it is treatable!)* since we lost Wendy. Through her we have reached out past our pain, past the stigma that is attached to this type of death. We have tried to offer friendship and caring to others that have found themselves in this unfortunate situation, feeling so desolate that there is no way out but death. *(You can read a few of the many posts I saved which are featured in chapter eleven)* This is **not** true there is help; there are people that care and I am one of them!

Where are we right now at this moment you may wonder? We are sad for the loss not only of our daughter and all that she would have contributed to this world, but for the continuing suicides that seem to happen on a daily basis. You don't hear about all of them. You usually hear about the ones that cause serious devastation and wreak havoc among the population, and with the advent of social media, this has become an even bigger problem, but you don't often hear about the ones that die alone and away from the crowds and the media and yet, these things are happening far too often in our Country and around the world.

To bolster this point I have included a small portion of an article from the American Psychological Association by Kirsten Weir from March 2019, Vol 50, No. 3 and page 24, the article is entitled:

"Worrying trends in U.S. suicide Rates"

She writes *"The suicide rate increased 33 percent from 1999 through 2017, from 10.5 to 14 suicides per 100,000 people (NCHS Data Brief No. 330, November 2018). Rates have increased more sharply since 2006. Suicide ranks as the fourth leading cause of death for people ages 35 to 54, and the second for 10- to 34-year-olds. It remains the 10th leading cause of death overall.* This was the only silver lining in the article. *"But it's a different story in other parts of the world. Over roughly the same period, other countries have seen rates fall, including Japan, China, Russia and most of Western Europe. What is going wrong on our shores—and what lessons can we import from elsewhere?"*

"Pinpointing the reasons that suicide rates rise or fall is challenging in part because the causes of suicide are complex. Risk factors include health factors (such as depression, substance use problems, serious mental illness and serious physical health conditions including pain), environmental factors (such as access to lethal means and stressful life events including divorce, unemployment, relationship problems or financial crisis) and historical

*factors (including previous suicide attempts, a family
history of suicide and a history of childhood abuse or
trauma). At the individual level, there is never a single
cause of suicide. There are always multiple risk factors,"
says Christine Moutier, MD, chief medical officer of the
American Foundation for Suicide Prevention. "That
confluence of multiple risk factors makes it a trickier
business to explain a population-level rise."*

And that silver lining really isn't great news because the
suicide rate in other Countries is well above ours to begin
with sadly.

I had a call from one of my daughter's dear friends from
high school, let's call him Bob. He has been having mental
health problems since graduating from school in 1995 and
has called me off and on. He has asked permission to visit
us time and again, and it is always granted, but he has of
yet never come by. One night he admitted that he had just
spent over a month in the hospital for his problems, and
his doctor told him that he needs to visit Wendy at her
final resting place to say goodbye. I agreed that it was a
good idea and told him exactly where she was in the
cemetery in case he didn't have the courage to come here
first. I want so badly to help this fellow out as Wendy did
throughout her high school years. Bob, if you ever read
this, we are here for you and that is a promise! Often what
it takes is simply being there for someone and helping
them wade through the sorrow and despair that this world
hands out at times. Not a day goes by that I don't think
about my daughter and see the light that she carried for
so long. On many levels she still does, only now it's
through me, a handful of her friends, and as you can see

as you read this book, Pastor Al. On a side note, Bob did make it over to the cemetery and left a little pink bear with a note. I sincerely hope that he is healing and on a good path. We put the bear in Wendy's room to remind us to always pray for Bob.

I have taken a long look back at the last two years and nine months and realize that a deep sadness still resides within me. I can go out amongst the population and they may never know what lies inside the depths of my soul. We still live in the same house, have the same furniture, same pets, same everything, except one car *(had to get rid of my other one-too many memories)*. However, it's not the same because it is lonelier. It is quieter and probably always will be, our new *"normal"* as I mentioned before. In the beginning, it was a struggle to even get up to turn a light switch on. The *"why's"* and *"would have's"* were with me always. Many of those are gone now as I know that I will never; *(in this lifetime)* receive the answers that I sought. I also know they will not make a difference in the outcome of my life at this point. *(Although I am deeply grateful for the difference Wendy has made in the lives of others)* I can only continue to look ahead with the peace I have received from the Lord within my soul and heart. Some days it comes easily, other days it is not so easy and I struggle still, but I know letting the Lord have control of my life has given me a peace that I had not found since this tragedy. Bill and I went to church for the first time in many years this Sunday and it was very comforting to know that there are others who will accept us, hurts and all. How many of you have turned, not only from God, but from people? I know that we had and in the people department still do at times. We have now let the Lord into our lives and what a comfort He is....I know in my heart of hearts that He is comforting my daughter, and that one day we will be together again. For now, I try my very best to help the ones that appear either in person or through Wendy's page, and there have been many as you will read just a few of those comments in chapter eleven. Here is a wonderful piece from a friend in Florida.

"Older Grief"
Written by Linda Zelenka

Older grief is gentler; it's about sudden tears swept by a stand of music.

It's about haunting echoes of first pain, at anniversaries.

It's about feeling her presence for an instant one day while I'm dusting her room.

Its' about early pictures that invite me to hold her in my arms again.

Its' about memories blown in on wisps of wood smoke and sea scent.

Older grief is about aching in gentler ways, rarer longing, less engulfing fire.

Older grief is about searing pain wrought into tenderness.

Fast forward to November 12, 2015. 19 years alive and yet 19 years gone; so hard to believe! Wendy we miss you each and every day. Time seems to be flying along, and that is alright. We have made plenty of mistakes along the way, but you dear girl, were never one of them. It is still so hard to grasp the reality that you are no longer here. We were truly blessed with such a wondrous young lady that bestowed so much warmth in this cold, hard world. It has been a tough year, with lots of changes as we grow older and some hard choices to make. We are contemplating actually selling the farm and moving on, not sure where or how yet, but we are leaving our options open. I am having a hard time thinking that I could not just walk across the road to visit *(Wendy's headstone is in the Cemetery just diagonally across the street from us)* or drive by on my way somewhere. I know we both miss you so much. You were such a bright light and kept us moving along.

Now, it is just necessity that keeps us moving and, sometimes grumpily so. We finally got around to updating your stone and painted the words on the back that mean so much to both of us – *"Our Shining Star, Yesterday, Today and Forever".* They are readable now and let the visitors know just how we feel about our girl, Wendy! We managed to take a vacation that was really fabulous. We went to Mt. Airy, North Carolina, *(actually it is Andy Griffith's Mayberry).* We had a grand time there with the visits to the Mayberry memorabilia and visited some great wineries in the mountains. We drove through Skyline Drive and remembered when we all went that way to Virginia Beach so many years ago with you. That was a wonderful vacation and it is very memorable. We continued our journey onto Virginia and visited our dear and good friends, the Stewart's, who were gracious enough to put us up for the night. It was an honor to be able to attend their bible study on Mark and meet some of the members that attend Al's church. Sometimes I think memories will wear out if we take them out too much, but the really good ones, never wear out, they become bittersweet on some level, but are precious to our lives. So many of their friends are doing so well and we appreciate the opportunities to catch a glimpse into their lives. Yes, it makes me wonder and makes me sad sometimes too. I often wonder about how your life would have been my dear daughter. I know our lives would have been different if you were still here, but that was not meant to be. At times, I grasp the pain that you must have been living with and am sorry that you were unable to reach out. These days now often make us both tired and ready for the next world. But, we keep on trying. I feel like you are with us many times; and it helps us one step at a time. We are trying to keep up the good fight, and we know that the finish line is getting nearer each day and we will be ready when the day comes for us to be reunited. My darling daughter if I knew your inner pain, I could of, and certainly would of helped anyway I could.

I hope and pray that you found your step-grandma, Norene Spear. We finally found her grave again and made sure we went and planted some spring bulbs. You have many people that loved you that have gone on to the next world and I hope you have all found each other, along with our wonderful God, whom promises eternal life to those who love Him and to those who suffered as you did. This year has been a year of sadness for loss of people, friends at work, changes in physical challenges, but also a year of finding some true friends and sharing when we can, where we can. Next year will be hard, as you will have been gone longer than you were here. How is that possible? It makes me so sad and so few really speak about it to us any longer. I understand, it is like a cut that scabs over and heals, but when it is your child, it never heals entirely, it scars deeply. And with that, we still try to find the joy in the rainbow, the lake, and the fall leaves that were very nice this past year.

We enjoy our small garden, flowers, and the porches that take in the summer breezes and wonderful fresh cut grass smells, along with the farmer's hay cutting, and sometimes the scent of manure that gets spread on the fields. There is joy and sadness in all of us, all the time it seems, but we have been able to bear more of it quietly these days. Wait for us! We miss you, we love you………!!!!!!!!!

Wendy in White, 1995

Chapter Six
Conversion

(Words from Rev. Al)

I was a bi-vocational Pastor in 2000 when I began to converse via email with Sharon. After many conversations *(many of which were gut wrenching to be honest, but let me say that the Lord was not only at work in Bill and Sharon, but He was at work in me as well, especially when it came to my emotions),* I made the commitment to visit them in person and to offer what I could for them to obtain some of the healing, enrichment and peace of mind that I knew only God could give them. There is a wonderful promise that Jesus made, first to His disciples when He told them He would soon be *"going away".* And that offer of peace is also for us, yes, you and me. I knew Jesus was offering this very same peace to Sharon and Bill. We find this offer in John chapter 14 and verse 27 *"Peace I leave with you. My peace I give to you. I do not give to you as the world gives. Don't let your heart be troubled or fearful."* That was the peace I desired to bring to their broken hearts.

Well with that I got out my map *(no GPS in those days, lol)* and saw that they were roughly 451 miles away. I believe it was a Tuesday or Wednesday when I asked Sharon what time her and Bill got home from work on Friday's. She told me they got home around 4 pm. I said that I was coming that Friday and that I'd be pulling into her yard right around 4 pm. Let's just say, she was surprised to say the least! Friday morning I jumped into my car and drove west along rt. 84 until I came to rt. 17/86 in NY State, not all that far from where the Woodstock festival took place back in '69. Then it was on through little towns and bigger cities along rt. 17, like Binghamton and Elmira. Then, all the way out to Jamestown, the birthplace of Lucille Ball on the banks of the Chautauqua Lake before getting into Pennsylvania along the shores of Lake Erie. Then across to the Ohio border and up rt. 11, dubbed *"the highway to nowhere"*, leading up to Ashtabula County. Rt. 11 was dubbed that because the steel that was going to be shipped down that highway never materialized, and so you won't pass all that many cars even to this day.

At around 4 pm Friday afternoon, I pulled in and we began to get acquainted in person instead of the previous long distance relationship of phone calls and emails. I think I can say with abject certainty that we all bonded in that first hour or so. And we were all brought together that day due to Wendy's loss. It would be fair to say that although she was not with us in the physical sense, she clearly was in a spiritual sense; in short, God was using her, even though she wasn't there with us! An amazing thing happened to us that 1st night; something I have never had happen before or since and trust me, I like food so I eat at a lot of places and never had a server do what this young lady did that night. I asked Bill and Sharon where their favorite restaurant was, and they told me of a place along Lake Erie called *"Lou's Billow Beach"*. Sharon made reservations and we headed out a few hours later for

Lou's. Shortly after being seated, our waitress, a young lady came over to our table and began to write her name on a small folded paper, she then placed it on the center of the table and said the following........ *"I'm here to serve you tonight and my name is Wendy"*....... Can you believe that? Needless to say, we could barely believe what we had just heard. Friends, there is absolutely no way that could have been a coincidence. For at that very moment, Bill, Sharon and I were having a difficult discussion about *"where Wendy was"* due to what happened. This was something that Sharon wanted to know above all else. As a Pastor of the Gospel and one who tries to be intentional about hearing the Holy Spirit, it was very clear to me that this was a message from God Himself saying *"Bill and especially Sharon, can you trust me that I have all things under control, including Wendy's whereabouts".* In fact, the next day as we walked along the banks of Lake Erie, we received another sign. This one was not as dramatic, but it was another reminder of God's goodness and faithfulness. A man walked by with a hat that had *"OWU"* on it. That was Wendy's College, Ohio Wesleyan University which is located some 4 plus hours from where we stood.

Those who know me know I live to be used by God and to have *"divine appointments",* but I must say that night at the Restaurant, and my meeting Bill and Sharon, and having become close and dear friends has truly been one of the most dramatic and powerful divine appointments I will ever have. I can honestly say that beauty did indeed come out of devastation and ashes. It was a phenomenal weekend and was most certainly the catalyst in leading Bill and Sharon back on the path of serving Jesus Christ as their personal Lord and Savior. Before I returned to my home state of Connecticut, we spent some time driving around Geneva looking at various churches. I spotted one; Peoples Christian Missionary Alliance Church and pointed out that we should go inside and meet the Pastor, which we did! *(I want to give a personal thanks to Pastor Walker, and the entire Congregation of those days for helping my dear friends during crucial early years of their new walk with the Lord Jesus Christ)* Bill & Sharon did search around a bit, but ended up after a few weeks attending the Church. It lasted for well over 5 years and the Church not only embraced Bill & Sharon, but the memory of Wendy as well. It is a very calming, wonderful feeling to know that you can have Jesus in your corner no matter what difficulties you will face in your life.

Does it make it totally smooth sailing? Absolutely not, but it sure gives the heart peace and assurance when needed! Last, I wanted to add this as well. With Bill's passing in April of 2018, it was an honor for me to travel back to Geneva, Ohio to do Bill's Eulogy and service with the help of her local Church, Eagleville Bible Church. I saw and continue to see, without any reservation, that while it's certainly still hard for her, Sharon has been a shining example of the work that Christ does in helping a person cope with such losses. It truly makes me wonder how it is possible that people are able to get by without the help of their Creator. Of course, we know that it is statistically clear that people get by with things that do not satisfy or last and are, in fact, destructive. Alcohol, drugs and isolation among others, which can only lead to utter despair, serious health issues, and depression.

Look to the Savior friends, who stands at the door of our hearts and declares the following in Revelation 3:20 the following: *"See! I stand at the door and knock. If anyone hears my voice and opens the door, I will come in to him and eat with him, and he with me"*.

Chapter Seven
Stigma and the Blame Game

(Words from Rev. Al)

In the next chapter *"Things to Consider",* Sharon will use a very disturbing word for those who have lost a loved one who took their own life. That word is *"stigma".* Sharon also writes in the next chapter about the fact that depression is very real. There are people whom for whatever reason, chemical or perhaps circumstantial are prone to depression. In this case, if you've gotten this far I am sure by now that you can fully understand why Wendy was suffering inside. Things happened to her which *"rocked her world".* Unfortunately, this world can and often is a very cruel place, especially for those who have tender or gentle souls.

So, you may ask, what is the stigma? Well I'll liken it this way. As a Pastor having lived in *"Church world"* all these years, it's sadly become almost commonplace that when a young child entering their teens begins to fall away from their faith. Almost instantly, rumors about the parents begin to filter their way through the Congregation. Things like, *"what did they do to cause their child to fall away?"* or perhaps something along these lines, *"you know they (the parents) were just too busy and they didn't invest in their child".* If I may quote Solomon, the writer of the book of Ecclesiastes, *"this is an evil I have seen under the sun".*

Friends, please hear me, other than starting such rumors which is downright cruel, it's often **not** the case! Consider the following righteous Biblical giants and figures whose children rebelled. Samuel was a very godly man and Prophet before God, yet here's what the Bible says of his sons: 1 Samuel 8:1-3 *When Samuel grew old, he appointed his sons as judges over Israel. 2 His firstborn son's name was Joel and his second was Abijah. They were judges in Beer-sheba. 3 However, his sons did not walk in his ways—they turned toward dishonest profit, took bribes, and perverted justice.* And what about King Jehoshaphat's son who also became King? Here's what the Bible tells us about this son of a godly King. We are told that Jehoram is remembered as one of the most decidedly wicked Kings in Judah's history. You can read about Jehoram in; 2 Kings 8:16-24 and 2 Chronicles 21.

What can we make of the first family? Was it not Adam's son Cain who killed his brother Abel? Yes, we can all agree that Adam did indeed sin, but it is clear that going forward he taught righteousness. How else would Abel have been able to bring an acceptable offering before the Lord? So, it would only make sense that Cain chose to rebel. In these three cases, should we now go ahead and throw Samuel, Jehosaphat and Adam *"under the bus"* for the actions of their children? I think you know the answer. I would submit that one of the most distorted and untruthful sayings are this, *"the acorn doesn't fall far from the tree".* As we have seen, and believe me that I can give many more examples, never was there a saying so misleading than that one! Bottom line, **when a child takes their life, never assume it's the parents fault.** As in the case of Bill and Sharon, they were as shocked as anyone. They were as caught off-guard as anyone else. Blaming the parents is simply a way to explain or make sense of such a situation to ease a person's mind from having to consider the reality that this does happen. Sadly it happens quite regularly around the world as well as in our own Country.

I'm not going to put up any statistics here, but it's been a problem since the beginning of time. Thinking such a thing helps us as humans to have an explanation, when the truth is that, all too often there really isn't one. I recently read about a young college student who by all outward appearances was happy and fulfilled. In reading the article, one could easily see she clearly came from a loving family.

While at college in the greater San Francisco area, one afternoon, she drove her car over the Golden Gate Bridge. She then parked it and began to walk along the rail. In the general place she stopped, parents and citizens have been advocating for years to place a suicide barrier on the rail, which, even at the time of this writing *(2019)* has fallen on deaf ears. I am happy to give this update in 2020. The Suicide Deterrent System, also known as the SDS, is being constructed to keep people from jumping off the Golden Gate Bridge. The Net will be placed 20 feet below the sidewalk, extending 20 feet out from the Bridge. This design was chosen through a public process which solicited input from the community. The selected design allows open, scenic vistas to remain intact, while preventing anyone from easily jumping to the water below. Once she got to that specific dangerous point, she climbed up easily and threw herself over the bridge into the frigid waters some 150 plus feet below to her own death. Her father has started an outreach to those who have lost their children to suicide, as well as to the many others whose children jumped from that very same bridge. And as you read my update, their tireless efforts are now paying off with the construction of the SDS on the bridge. This serves as a model for those of us concerned about suicide to be a strong advocate in our Communities, talk to legislators, mental health professionals and take a public stand, in short, have an impact in your sphere of influence.

I was in tears reading this story, it touched the same way Wendy's story did. He had NO clue whatsoever what his daughter was feeling or what she was about to do. The devastation came through each word he wrote right off the page. I could literally feel it. Friends, I beseech you in the name of the Lord to **never** wag or point your finger at any parent who's lost their child this way. Here's what I do recommend.

Take the hard road, the road to the second mile, if you will. Listen to them, do your best to walk in their shoes before you judge them, or even feel any need to judge them! Understand this truth……it could happen to anyone who is a parent. My prayer is this, *"God, may we never add one ounce of pain to a parent who has already suffered to their breaking point, help us to never be that ignorant in Jesus name"*……..Amen.

Chapter Eight
Things to Consider

Wendy running track for Geneva High School

If you have a heart and desire to help and try to understand those of us who have gone, or are going through life altering events. I want to give you some important things to consider in this chapter, as you reach out to those hurting.

What would have happened if nineteen years ago, the Lord smiled down on you and said: *"I am going to entrust you with a beautiful daughter. She will be full of love and laughter. She will brighten your lives in countless ways. You will love her to the depths of your soul. She will grow to become a curious and vivacious child. Others will notice her. She will be admired and well-liked by her peers. Her teachers, other parents, indeed, her entire community, will be touched by her spirited presence in their lives, including even those at a distance. Oh, there is one more thing. This beautiful child I am bringing her Home without warning, long before you believe you are ready to part with her."*

Would I, could I have abided by those rules? Yes, if I had to do it all over again and knew the consequences of having this precious soul in our midst, I would have run headlong to begin again. Knowing that I cannot do this, please Lord Keep my child safe within your loving arms until that day we are to be reunited.

First are Holidays/Special Days, we begin dreading the holidays shortly after our child dies. A birthday or anniversary coming up soon scares us, but not like the anticipation of Thanksgiving or Christmas does. We expend mountains of energy dreading and fearing these special times. We either *"awfulize"* how we're going to feel-- painting dreadful mental pictures of searing, unbearable pain, hysterical reactions or just plain fading away. We absolutely refuse to allow our minds to even touch on thoughts of these days. Either way, the dread and fear can overwhelm us.

Now we know that it is perfectly normal to be afraid of what we think might happen. Our reaction to the death of our child is so unlike anything we ever expected that we are sure that the holidays are going to be even worse. Let me reassure you, just as your grief reactions are normal, so is your fear.

Second, remember that by the time the day arrives, you have completed most of the hard work of the holidays. It's in the doing of holiday tasks that the pain lies, so, by the time the day arrives, the real work is over. The need to change some traditions may be in the offing and help to allow you to manage your emotions. No one says you have to bake cookies or do elaborate preparations for whatever the day may bring. The day will still go on and it will start to become your new normal.

Third, know each day is only <u>twenty four hours long</u>. You'll get through it like you get through any other day, some are harder, and some are easier. This is the good news and the bad news.

Last, take charge of your fear. Tell yourself that it is okay to have any emotion you want about the holidays. Make concrete plans for your behavior. Give yourself permission to cry or scream, or even pull the covers over your head if you feel like it. Make contingent plans that you can put into practice if you cannot handle a situation.
The loss of your child is the absolute worst thing that could ever happen to you. You are not alone. There are literally thousands walking down the same road. Don't be afraid to reach out and ask for help! For one, I am with you. With that said, please know that you have a friend in me. If you can find no one else to share these feelings with, I am usually but a keystroke away and I understand and care. I've been there my friend.

Chapter Nine
Poems & Prose

WE'RE ALIKE, YOU AND I;
Written by Judy Dickey

We're alike, you and I.
We've never met
Our faces would be those of strangers if we met
We would barely perceive the other's presence
If we passed on our walk through the mists
We're unknown to each other
Until the terrible words have been spoken
"MY CHILD DIED"
We're alike, you and I
We measure time in seconds and eternities
We try to go forward to yesterday
Tomorrows are for the whole people,
And we are incomplete now
The tears after a time turn inward
To become invisible to all save you and me
Our souls are rumpled from wrestling with demons.
And doubts and unanswerable prayers.
"GIVE ME BACK MY CHILD"
We're alike, you and I.
The tears that run down your face are my tears
And the wound in your soul is my pain too.
We need time, but time is our enemy
For it carries us farther and farther
From our lost child
And we cry out;
"HELP ME"

We're alike, you and I.
And we need each other
Don't turn away, but give me your hand
And for a time we can cease to be strangers
And become what we truly are,
A family closer than blood.
United by a bond that was forced upon us---
But a bond that can make us stronger,
Still wounded and not to sure,
But stronger for our sorrows are shared.

"We Need Not Walk Alone"
Heaven's Child

Written by Susan Marie Jeavons *(she was part of the EMT group and wrote this for Wendy after they could not save her)*

God sent a child from heaven
To make us laugh and smile,
But she was only with us,
For such a little while.

She seemed so very happy,
So full of life and pride,
Now we'll never know the feelings,
She kept hidden deep inside.

For one day God came and took her,
And carried her a way,
To be with Him in heaven,
Oh Lord we only pray.

That she knew how proud we were,
How much we loved her so,
Now she's heaven's child.
Yes in my heart I know.

She's smiling down upon us,
And prays we understand,
She's reaching down with angel wings,
To gently hold our hands.

She whispers that she loved us,
As her halo glows so bright,
Now a new star up in heaven,
Will shine on us tonight!

The Elephant in the Room
Written by Terry Katterling

There's an elephant in the room.
It is large and squatting, so it is hard to get around
it.
Yet we squeeze by with How are you and I'm fine.
And a thousand other forms of trivial chatter.

We talk about the weather.
We talk about work.
We talk about everything else – except the elephant
in the room.
There's an elephant in the room.

We all know it is there.
We are all thinking about the elephant as we talk.

It is constantly on our minds.
For you see, it is a very large elephant.

But, we do not talk about the elephant in the room.
Oh, please, say her name.
Oh, please, say Wendy again.
Oh, please, let's talk about the elephant in the room.

For if we talk about her death,
perhaps we can talk about her life.
Can I say Wendy and not have you look away?
For, if I cannot, you are leaving me
Alone.......in a room......with an elephant.....

(Any name may be substituted)

Country Cemetery
~Author Unknown

In a quiet country cemetery,

Where the gentle breezes blow,

Lays my daughter I love so dearly;

She died a few years ago.

Her resting place I visit,

Placing flowers there with care,

But no one knows my heartache,

When I turn to leave them there.

Though her smile is gone forever,

And her hands I cannot touch,

Still I have so many memories

Of the daughter I loved so much.

Her memory is my keepsake,

With which I will never part.

God has her in His keeping;

I have her in my heart.

Tears Are the Proof of Life
Author Unknown

"How long will the pain last a broken-hearted mourner asked me?". "All the rest of your life," I had to answer truthfully. We never quite forget. No matter how many years pass we remember. The loss of a loved one is like a major operation; part of us is removed and we have a scar for the rest of our lives. This does not mean that the pain continues at the same intensity. There is a short while at first, when we hardly believe it; it is rather like when we cut our hand. We see the blood flowing, but the pain has not set in yet. So when we are bereaved, there is a short while before the pain hits us. But when it does, it is massive in its effect. Grief is shattering.

Then the wound begins to heal. It is like going through a dark tunnel. Occasionally we glimpse a bit of light up ahead, then we lose sight of it awhile, and then see it again, and one day we merge into the light. We are able to laugh, to care, to live. The wound is healed so to speak. The stitches are taken out, and we are whole again.

But not quite. The scar is still there, and the scar tissue, too. As the years go by, we manage. There are things to do, people to care for, and tasks that call for full attention. But the pain is still there, not far below the surface. We see a face that looks familiar, hear a voice that has echoes, see a photograph in someone's album, see a landscape that once we saw together, and it as though the knife were in the wound again.

But not so painfully, and mixed with joy, too. Because remembering a happy time is not all sorrow; it brings back happiness with it. As a matter of fact, we even seek such moments in bittersweet remembrance. We have our religious memories and our memorial days, and our visits to the cemetery. And though these bring back the pain, they bring back memories of joy as well.

How long will the pains last? All the rest of your life. But the thing to remember is that not only the pain will last, but the blessed memories as well. Tears are the proof of life. The more love, the more tears. If this were true, then how could we ever ask that the pain cease altogether? For then the memory of love would go with it. The pain of grief is the price we pay for love.

Autumn of My Life
Written by Sharon Bryant

In the autumn of my life
Now that the days are finally here
I think about what could have been
Instead of what was, all these years

My hair is turning white
like a new fallen snow
yet my heart still remembers
When life was all aglow

Now that I am older
with more than half my life passed by
I think of things I wish I'd done
and never question why

I think of how some are so lucky
That nothing bad every came into their life
how some marriages lasted a lifetime
For certain husbands and wives

I think of what I could have done
to change the path I walked
would I be someone different
than just the old woman who types and talks?

I think about a little girl
I gave birth to long ago
and though I loved with all my heart
her life with me for very long, was not to be so

I think about the raindrops
on a hot summer day

I think of how tears are
an endless storm today

I think of how many lives
have come into my own
and how things I once cared about
are not important as I now know

I think of what I can do
before I leave this earthly life
to leave something good behind
for bereaved husbands and wives

I think about heaven
and how fast it takes to get there
I think, Can I prove it exists
to parents everywhere?

I think about my own heart
and the years I've had to grieve
it never seems it could have happened
So many years ago, to me

Love is yesterday,
Today and tomorrow too
I'll never let go of my heart
Until my time is spent with you

My autumn years are now here
And there's nothing that I can do
But patiently wait my turn
And I once again get to hold you

I'll imagine that day
and what a Glory it will be

When God calls my name
into eternity with Him, you and me

So wait my child for me
the years are ticking fast away
my autumn years have arrived
I'll be with you again someday.......

One Taken To Heart.....for Wendy
Written by Sara Holbook, November 15, 1996

A book, so much a part of our lives, seems lost.
Fallen, somewhere out of place. We drag about the
house in heavy shoes, examining the empty rooms.

We open the blinds, wash our eyes and search the
shelf for answers, thinking, what could we have done
with that book, where did we see it last?

 Could a book just wander off like that?

Questions to throw at the moon while standing,
round in the shadows, remembering the story, the
story. Remember the time? The page? The chapter?
Remember?

Remember the smile?

A book can get lost, disappear, or simply fall to
pieces, but a story plays forever once we've taken it
to heart. And for the rest of what each of us will
know of eternity, even when, barehanded, we drag
about the house in heavy shoes.

Wash our eyes and search the shelf for answers, the story will survive to coax us from the empty room, back into the moonlight. A sister, teaching us to dance.

This prose above was written three days after Wendy passed away by one of Wendy's sorority sisters' mom, Sara Holbrook. She refers to the dancing at the end, because Wendy taught them to do a line dance that she learned when she was in a Miss Grapette pageant in Geneva. And this young lady also told of this instance in the memorial service that followed at OWU.

Last, this is a song that Pastor Al wrote a few years after he met us about Wendy, as well as all those considering taking their lives. He is a songwriter and drummer. This song is available to anyone who would like it at no cost, simply write to Pastor Al at his PO Box, which is found on page 137, and he will be glad to send it to you via email.

"Blue Gray Sky / Wendy's Song"
Words & Music by Al Stewart,
© 2003 Poboy Music.

Alone, you're feeling all alone, out of any zone, any zone.   Deep down inside, your trying to hide, your inner wild ride, wild ride.

Don't know what to do, or who will see ya through, you totally withdrew, you withdrew.   Looking up you cry, you ask yourself why, and think that you must die, you must die

Blue Gray Sky, Blue Gray Sky, Makes Me Wonder
Why, Makes Me Wonder Why

Your planning your demise, your letter's no surprise,
no surprise.   But you try to see the truth, from your
isolation booth, isolation booth.   You see people
really care, they've always been there, they've been
there.   Your friends & family, are part of life's key,
part of life's key.

Blue Gray Sky, Blue Gray Sky, Makes Me Wonder
Why, Makes Me Wonder Why

Blue Gray Sky, Blue Gray Sky, Makes Me Wonder
Why, Makes Me Wonder Why

Now how can they go on, when part of them is gone.
Not an easy thing to do, many have followed too.
So please don't take your life, go on to live another
day.   Remember help's okay, it's the only way

 Blue Gray Sky, Blue Gray Sky, Makes Me Wonder
Why, Makes Me Wonder Why

Why she ever felt this way, with so much more to
say, so get the help you need, it's not time to succeed.
Hold your head up high, and look into the sky, and you will
see your Son shine through your Blue Gray Sky, your Blue
Gray Sky, through your Blue Gray Sky.

The last picture we had together. Taken at the OWU campus. If we had only known......

Chapter Ten
Valuable Resources

RED FLAGS

THE FOLLOWING CAN BE SIGNS OF DEPRESSION-AND POSSIBLE SUICIDE some may think it is just teenage angst, but it is worth noting changes and acting appropriately!

• **Personality changes:** withdrawal from friends and family; anxiety; hyperactivity; restlessness; extreme fatigue; apathy

• **Behavioral changes:** Inability to concentrate in school or routine tasks; heavy or increased use of drugs or alcohol.

• **Physical problems:** insomnia or oversleeping; nightmares; loss of appetite or overeating; scratches or marks on the body, particularly at the wrists and neck; continual stomach pain that stems from anxiety.

• **Low self-esteem:** worthlessness; overwhelming guilt; self-hatred; anger with the world.

• **No hope for future:** belief that things will never change.

• **Things to watch for:** verbal or written expressions of suicide; themes of death in music, art, speech, or writing;

giving away favorite things; statements that he/she will not be missed if gone.

Suicide Helplines; Know someone who needs help? The organizations listed below can provide information, resources, or referral services.

- **National Suicide Prevention Lifeline: 800-273-8255 - www.suicidepreventionlifeline.org**

- **American Foundation For Suicide Prevention *(aka SPAN)*: www.afsp.org**

- **National Depression Screening Day – October 10 www.nationaltoday.com/national-depression-screening-day**

- **Suicide Prevention - HelpGuide.org**

  www.helpguide.org/articles/suicide-prevention/...

Suicide Prevention starts with recognizing the warning signs and taking them seriously. If you think a friend or family member is considering suicide, there's plenty you can do to help save a life.

Roughly 40 million adults in the U.S. struggle with depression or anxiety. Not to mention the family, friends and coworkers that are also impacted. National Depression Screening Day is held annually on October 10th. It's important for many reasons. First, it can help people make an informed diagnosis. It also drags depression out of the darkness.

- **The National Alliance For The Mentally Ill: 1-800-950-NAMI: www.nami.org**

- **American Association Of Suicidology: www.suicidology.org**

At the end of chapter thirteen, Sharon has a list of book's she highly recommends that have been helpful to her throughout the years.

Chapter Eleven
People Reaching Out / Guestbook Entries

Bill's Favorite Picture of Wendy

The following are guestbook entries from Wendy's website over the years. Many of them are so heartfelt I had the need to share their thoughts and prayers with those of you who have been willing to read Wendy, Bill and my story here. From time to time as I read these, I take solace in knowing we've helped others along the way.

Name: R** Pr****
Website: Ber** Church
Referred by: From a Friend
From: Dahonega, GA
Time: 1999-11-11 01:50:11
Comments: Shar, So sorry to learn of your loss. Judging by the web pages you reference, you have gotten some good support. As a pastor and counselor I have been there with dear friends more often than I wish. As a father of a 16 year old daughter and two sons 13 and 10 I feel that I can in some way empathize with your loss, but still having all three of mine, I can never know how you feel. Your address and request for visits was forwarded by a good friend and member of our church. I am passing it on to most in my address book as well. I am sure that many have prayed for you and your husband since the loss and you may rest assured that more will be praying for you now. Rev. Ra***** P***** Berea Baptist Church Dahlonega, GA www.be****church.org

---

Name: S** S******
Website:
Referred by: AngelFire
From: Canada
Time: 1999-11-11 00:36:17
Comments: My thoughts are with you at this very difficult time. Our first year is soon approaching on November 20 1999. A day I would like to forget but will always remember. We have lost one of Gods precious gifts. May our lives heal someday somehow. I am truly sorry for your loss. For I do know what you are going through. Take care of yourself. I will be thinking

of you. I will say a little prayer for the both of us and for our dear children Wendy and Jonathan Love S**

Name: P**
Website: My Memorials
Referred by: From a Friend
From: CT
Time: 1999-11-10 13:24:31
Comments: What a wonderful tribute to your daughter, my son took his own life at 16, I don't know if I could write his story, this was in 81 and I had no one to talk to, no one to ask the questions, and lived with the horror alone, God Bless you, P**

Name: Na*** Ma*****
Website: What Could have Been....What Wasn't
Referred by: From a Friend
From: Cherry Hill, NJ
Time: 1999-11-10 10:44:23
Comments: OH Shar.....Not a day goes by, I don't think of our girls. 3 years of hell and it does seem like yesterday : (God help us! I have taken the liberty of adding Wendy's site to J*** new site. I love you all so much and I wanted to do something special in memory of Wendy, so I have put her with her angel-sister) As, I know they soar together ..... Please contact me if you need to chat/vent , I am always here for you ! I mean this. You have done so much on Wendy's site; you bring much light to the taboo of suicide. Love ya Girlfriend, Love our girls and 1000 hugs to Bill. I am always here for you! With Love and Peace on this Journey, Nance Mom to J***.......God Loves our babies :)

Name: Ka****
Website: Wolf Whispers
Referred by: From a Friend
Name: No**** & N**** Bl*****
Website: Hugh's Final Home Page
Referred by: Just Surfed On In
From: Pearl City, HI
Time: 1999-11-09 16:25:03
Comments: There is no pain like the pain you experience when you lose a child; and if that loss is the result of suicide, it's multiplied a countless number of times. Our son departed this world by his own hand on June 3, 1999. We know the pain you're feeling and share it completely. The one thing we can be certain of is that both your daughter and our son now know each other sitting at the feet of God. Their pain and suffering have ended, as ours will, when we all meet again in Heaven. May God bless you all. Yours in pain and suffering. No**** & N**** Bl*****

Name: H****
Website:
Referred by: Just Surfed On In
From: Toronto, Canada
Time: 1999-11-06 17:33:29
Comments: This website made me very sad. I am a young female who suffers from very bad depression, I have attempted suicide and luckily did not succeed. Reading your story makes me realize the sadness one leaves behind in when something like this happens. I will try to keep this in mind. Thank you for sharing a very difficult story.

Name: K****** S******
Website: With One Voice
Referred by: From a Friend
From: Ohio
Time: 1999-10-04 05:26:08
Comments: Shar, Wendy was beautiful! I am thankful for her page so that others may read her story and know that suicide IS a reality. My thoughts and prayers are with you and your family. Hopefully one day soon our program will be throughout the country making a difference to many. With One Voice.....We Make a Difference!

Name: Br**** Mi******
Website:
Referred by: From a Friend
From: Ruston, Louisiana
Time: 1999-09-23 22:37:06
Comments: This is a great and sad memorial page, but it was exactly what I needed. I always imagine what it would be like to not live on Earth. I don't think I would ever commit suicide, but now day's people don't care how they make you feel or even what kind of impact they make on you. Society now has gotten horrible and I pray that it will get better every night. I will pray for the Throop family. And I hope they get through they're grief. I always think of it as she has gone on to a better place and does have to live through a lot of the pressure in society today. I thought this was an awesome memorial page and I think it will reach out to other teens. Hopefully it will make them think twice about suicide. If they see the grief and pain a family goes

through, I am almost certain they wouldn't do it. I know that I wouldn't. It is people like Mrs. Sharon Throop that can help to save lives. I will refer my friends and family to this memorial page. You never know as it might save someone's life. Bye, Love in Christ- Br**** Mi******

Name: K****
Website: In Memory of Jamie and Ashley
Referred by: From a Friend
From: SC
Time: 1999-09-05 21:54:26
Comments: Sharon, this is such a beautiful memorial for a beautiful daughter. Thank you especially for the Two Years, Nine Months page. It gives me hope that this terrible pain will ease a bit. Thank you for the welcome to Without You and for your encouragement. God Bless You.

Name: Ch***** Al****
Website: Don't know...it's not too good!
Referred by: From a Friend
From: Foxworth, Mississippi
Time: 1999-08-22 03:11:45
Comments: The time and loving devotion you have spent in order to create this wonderful tribute to your daughter is commendable. Though we will never understand what actually causes someone to take their life, it is not our place to judge. Only to be respectful and to honor the memories of those lives and what they contributed while they were here on earth. With memories, loved ones will always be with us and never forgotten.

Name: M**** St******
Website:
Referred by: Just Surfed On In
From: Guthrie Center, Iowa
Time: 1999-08-16 06:01:05
Comments: Sharon, You voiced *so* many of the thoughts I
have daily! It is *so* good that you and Bill have gone back to
church and to your relationship with our Savior! I truly don't
know how to walk this "path" without the help my faith gives
me, but know that my husband, Steve, must walk it without
that help.... You are a blessing to all who get to know you!
Thank you for your support at GP! Love, Me*** A***

Name: Dale Sunderlin II
Website:
Referred by: From a Friend
From: Geneva, OH
Time: 1999-07-08 02:34:24
Comments: I wanted to sign your guest book even though I
viewed this site on your PC. It took me a long time to put a lot
of the pain behind me and focus on the life I now have. Most of
that was because I didn't know her as I probably should have,
as I know she knew more about others than we knew of her.
I'm sure Wendy is proud, not only of her big brother but of her
wonderful mother, for having the courage to go beyond the pain
& help others to deal with their pain, also. Thanks for showing &
telling me things about Wendy I wouldn't have otherwise
known. Love, Dale (Will)

Name: Kr** M***
Website:
Referred by: From a Friend
From: Geneva, OH
Time: 2000-06-29 11:50:41
Comments: Sharon, I'm not sure if you remember me *(my last name was So****)* but I just want to thank you so much for this website. It took me a long time before I could go and visit Wendy's grave for the first time, but now I go every time I get a change to visit my home town. I used to go and sit and talk to her for a while by myself and the last time I was home I finally took my new husband to meet her. I live in Illinois right now because I'm in the Air Force and I am so thankful that I now have a place to go to visit her while I'm so far away. I miss her and I just wanted to let you know how thankful I am for what you have done in her memory. I have so many good memories of Wendy and our friendship and I will never let it fade. Kr** M***

Name: J**** F**
Website:
Referred by: From a Friend
From: Trumbull Township Ohio
Time: 2000-06-01 16:43:12
Comments: Sharon, I am not sure if you remember me or not. You may know my mother though, Jo*** F**. A friend that Wendy and I graduated with told me about this site last night and I am so glad she did. I remember when Wendy first came to school at Cork. She was always such a wonderful person.

When I found out what had happened to Wendy I too was in my second year of college but could not believe it. Wendy was the last person that would have come to mind to do such a thing. But I know how people who are so severely depressed can hide their true feelings so well. My mom, who is also one of my Best Friends, suffers from severe depression. Her doctors can't seem to find the right combination of drugs for her. It is so scary for me. I pray every day that losing her the way you lost Wendy won't be the way that she leaves us. This is a wonderful web site and I am so glad I have visited it. I will check back every now and then to see any changes. Love J****

Name: An**** Gar*******
Website:
Referred by: Just Surfed On In
From: Chardon, OH
Time: 2000-05-23 21:16:14
Comments: Sharon and Bill, Wendy was such a beautiful person, not just on the outside, but on the inside as well. I went to school with her at Cork, and was also in Girl Scouts with her and St****, when Stacie's mom was our leader. I remember that Wendy and St**** coerced me into joining Girl Scouts when we were in fourth grade, since they said it was boring and would be more fun if they had more friends in it!! We grew apart in high school, just from different interests, and I always kind of felt bad that we lost touch. We were never best friends or anything, but Wendy was always such a fun person to hang out with and share some laughs!! Gosh, I never would have thought Wendy would do this to herself; she was never one to let anything get her down, no matter how bad it was. My heart goes out to you, her family. May God make each day easier for you.

Name: Ka*** Car******
Website:
Referred by: AngelFire
From: Geneva, Ohio
Time: 2000-05-19 21:35:26
Comments: I graduated from Geneva High School also, when I was a freshman Wendy was a senior, I loved that senior class everyone cared so much for the people around them. I still have so many friends from the 1995 graduation year. I was on classmates.com and saw Wendy's site. The tribute you have given her is beautiful. I am sorry to find out about this loss, she was a wonderful person. Ka*** Geneva High School Class of 1998.

Name: Shi***** L****
Website:
Referred by: Just Surfed On In
From: Oklahoma
Time: 2000-04-17 04:34:39
Comments: I lost my son, he committed suicide on 9/21/99 in his car with carbon monoxide, I have not been able to completely accept this as of yet, my heart and prayers are with you. May God Bless You, Shi***** L****

Name: K****
Website: Compassionate Friends – Ar***
Referred by: From a Friend

From: South Georgia
Time: 2000-03-26 22:32:00
Comments: Shar, I decided to stop by and visit Wendy --- came straight from the GP site here. This is a beautiful site. Each time I visit a site you have in memory of Wendy; I cannot help but feel the deep love you have for her. Wendy was very special, and she has a very special mommy. Love and peace, K****, Mother of Ar***

Name: Ka*** Ro******
Website:
Referred by: From a Friend
From: Ohio
Time: 2000-03-20 02:17:23
Comments: Sharon, This is an outstanding tribute to Wendy, an incredible person and a wonderful friend. All the pictures and antidotes bring back many memories, filled with both tears and smiles. I will always remember Wendy's laugh and her smile. She honestly had the most brilliant, beautiful smile. Wendy will forever be missed by all the people she touched, all who knew her. Together, you and Wendy are helping many others deal with the tragedies and hardships of this world, evident by reading all the entries in the guestbook. Thank you for all of your words of comfort and wisdom. Eternally, Wendy is in my thoughts and her family/friends are in my prayers. She is safe and happy once again; I truly believe this *(and take great comfort in it).* She will always live on as my shining star. Love you Wendy. Love always, Ka*** *(a friend and a sister of Wendy)*

Name: Chr******** K*****
Website:
Referred by: Just Surfed On In
From: Oxford, Oh
Time: 2000-02-28 21:54:44
Comments: I too am a survivor of suicide and appreciate your expressions of grief. I have dealt with my distant grief in a predictable way; I am a crisis hotline counselor. I will begin training in May to become a rape crisis counselor as well. I only bring this up to encourage anyone who this page, or tragedy, has touched to please find a way to help in your community. I only wish I could have been there for Wendy as well as countless of others a year. Please let's all make a difference. CWK

Name: T*** O****
Website:
Referred by: Just Surfed On In
From: Utah
Time: 2000-02-21 02:36:38
Comments: Sharon, I was browsing through all the pictures and Wendy caught my eye for some reason I just want you to know that you sharing your story about Wendy has made me look at life a little different thank you for sharing a part of you and your life with me! You're in my prayers.

Name: Sheldon
Website:
Referred by: Just Surfed On In
From: Toronto, Ontario, Canada
Time: 2000-02-21 00:40:06
Comments: just arrived at your site accidently...having a 19 year old daughter of my own....well...your site just hit me...I am truly sorry for your experience and heartache....I cannot imagine how you feel....I only hope that as time passes all your joy about your daughter will be what fills your heart...it is obvious you love her so much....my thoughts are with you...I just don't know what else to say...

Name: Ka********
Website: The Mar****
Referred by: Just Surfed On In
From: NC
Time: 2000-01-18 04:33:18
Comments: your daughter is so beautiful. I know that your heart aches that you could not help her. I have suffered from depression for almost 20 years and taken meds for the last 15, I still have my days when I don't know if I can make it through. There is nothing you can do for someone so depressed unless they want it. I have tried several times in my life and thank GOD I failed at that, just as I failed at living. God Bless you, and know that whatever was tormenting Wendy, she could not face it with or without any ones' help. She will forever be a beautiful Angel in GOD's Garden..........

Name: Mom *(Sharon)*
Website: Wendy's Memorial Pages
Referred by: From a Friend
From: Ohio
Time: 1999-12-16 11:43:42
Comments: For my dearest daughter.....I miss you more then you know, and some days are still a huge struggle w/o you here. My regrets could fill a football stadium and I am sorry for the pain that you felt and the fact that you could not see a way around it. If only, if only, if only..... I love you! Mom

Name: As**** P*****
Website:
Referred by: From a Friend
From: Dahlonega, Georgia
Time: 1999-11-18 22:00:27
Comments: I'm sorry about your daughter. I'm in tears right now. I'm 16 years old and a junior in high school. I can remember a few times when I've thought about suicide, but never seriously. When I start to think about it, I wonder who would miss me and what it would be like. I would never do it though, because I know I have friends and family who love me and no matter how hard life will get, I can get through it. I'm glad you wrote this page. I pray that many people my age will read it and be as touched by it as I was. God Bless, As****

Name: R** Ma****
From: Ft. Myers, Florida

Comments: I found this website five years ago when I googled my mother's name, P**** L** Ma***. This is the only place on the internet I could find anything from her; a message in this guestbook, dated April, 2000. She committed suicide in 2004. I've now lost an uncle, a brother and my mother to suicide.

This website has been a huge comfort to me since I was 15. Sometimes, while I was in high school, my mind would wander to dark places. Every time I'd come here and read about Wendy, I would read about the incredible amount of pain it caused you, the rest of your family and her friends. How one stupid decision that she made created a ripple effect that changed many other lives forever. I would be reminded of the pain my brothers suicide caused my mom and I, and the pain her suicide caused me. I realized that suicide doesn't make the pain someone feels go away it just pushes that pin onto the people that love you.

This website helped me resolve to never, ever, push that pain onto the people that I love. I haven't thought about suicide for a long time now. I just wanted to let you know that. You and Wendy have made a difference. _You've saved at least one life_.

Name: Mom

Comments; November 12, 2016 to our daughter today – We have been beyond sad this week thinking that you have been gone longer then you were here. We both miss you so much and wish you were here to help so many thru the trials and tribulations that this life requires. Our tears overflow and our hearts are heavy with the loss of you, even after all this time. I know many would say; what the heck – move on, but that is much easier said than done. If only goes thru our minds over the years and as we draw closer to the end it rings truer and truer. I do thank all the people that have kept you in their hearts and thoughts as well over these past 20 years. It means more then they know. So today you are missed, loved and never forgotten! Love Mom & Bill

---

Response email: From Ka*** her college friend written on 11/13/16.

Hello Mrs. Throop, I've thought about Wendy more time over the years than I can count and today 20 years later I've sat in silent remembrance and prayer several times. In so many ways I cannot believe 20 years have passed – my memories of her are still so fresh. Wendy has left an enormous mark on my life. My good friends, those who've I've met within the last 10-15 years, know of Wendy. She's truly been one of the greatest influencers of my life. **You mentioned in a post today that you wished that she'd be able to help others through life's trials and tribulations and I wanted to share that she has. She has, she helped me make it through several heartaches, which I worried were unbearable.** Her bright smile, her genuine kindness and her legacy lives on in places that unfortunately, you haven't had the chance to see. On this day of great sorrow I wanted to share a ray of light that still shines from dear, sweet Wendy. I hope knowing the positive influence she has had brings comfort on some level. Much love, Ka***

These are just a few of the hundreds of responses I received. They have meant the world to both Bill and I over the years and have helped to keep our paths moving forward. This is not to say that we do not hit bumps in the road as I've mentioned. That being said, I'm reminded what the book of Romans chapter 12:6-8 *(CSB Bible)* says about being encouraging amongst other things. *According to the grace given to us, we have different gifts: If prophecy, use it according to the proportion of one's faith; 7 if service, use it in service; if teaching, in teaching; 8 if exhorting, in exhortation; giving, with generosity; leading, with diligence; showing mercy, with cheerfulness.*

And further we read this in Romans 15:4. *(CSB Bible) For whatever was written in the past was written for our instruction, so that we may have hope through endurance and through the encouragement from the Scriptures.*

Chapter Twelve
Understanding Suicide

Both Sharon and I will divide this chapter. I will share first. In using the heading, *"understanding suicide"* the last thing I'm trying to be is pretentious. By no means do I think me, or really anyone else, has a *"corner"* so to speak on trying to understand why people take such a drastic action in deep, desperate times. Lord knows there are tons of theories out there on the subject, and I for one do not believe there is any one *"wise old man or woman,"* who can totally understand and explain suicide. The fact of the matter is that all we can do is look closely at each situation and try to surmise similar events and reoccurring behaviors that lead up to such an event. In this chapter Sharon, and I have done our best to do that from our experience, and I am a man who lives by the slogan, *"a man with an argument is no match for a man with experience"*.

Having said that, let me add that I must confess that despite being a Pastor, many people assume that being such, automatically makes you a good counselor. Unfortunately, that is often not the case. Most Pastors are pretty adept at Preaching, Teaching, Evangelizing, and offering support and encouragement, etc. However, I believe that Counseling is a whole different kettle of fish, if you will. The fact is, it doesn't come automatically with Ministry. Now, I have been pretty fortunate. Having been a Pastor for a long time, I have had the honor of helping many people, but there have been times where I have simply run into a brick wall with some folks. Now, as I mentioned, I do live by this motto *"a man with an argument is not match for a man with experience,"* and sadly in the area of dealing with suicide I have had more experiences then I desired. Like with Bill and Sharon, I have seen God bring beauty from ashes. I say all that to say this, I never hesitate to call or seek out the help of a clinically trained professional, and if you are a Pastor reading this, can I encourage you to do the same when needed, just as I have on a few occasions? Having said that, I want to talk about suicide, and specifically the misunderstanding of it that I have witnessed in the Body of Christ over many years.

For instance, many Christians believe that suicide is a very *"black and white"* issue. That if a person dies by it, they are fully destined for Hell. After all, isn't it, *"self-murder?"* To be honest, I believed that for many years as a committed Christian. I'm thankful that today I no longer believe that, so let me tell you what I do believe. First off, I believe it must be taken like the issue of divorce, **only** on a case by case basis. I have come to realize the truth that cancer can exist in a person's lungs, it can appear in a person's bones, basically, it can appear virtually anywhere in the human body, and I also believe that there are some people who suffer from what I can only term *"mind cancer".* As in the case of Wendy, look at what happened to her. There can be no question that a few events happened that caused her deep anxiety, attacked and ate at her self-worth. Only God knows what was in her mind and heart that lead up to that fateful day. In short, her circumstances were well out of the ordinary, it wasn't like she just traveled home and took her life for no apparent reason. She was taken advantage of. As a man, can I ever truly understand what that does to a women's feeling of self-worth or image? Can I be so bold as to declare that she is lost forever by ignoring the events that obviously lead up to that horrible day? What of the other people I have known who suffered similar circumstances and took their lives? Am I to likewise assume that it was nothing that pushed them over the edge to commit such an act? Now, I know many of my Christian friends are probably thinking of a passage I quoted in my Introduction, John 10:10 where Jesus said,

"A thief (Satan) comes only to steal, kill and destroy". Yes, I do believe the enemy is incredibly cunning and is unmatched in getting people to think that they are worthless and that life is not worth living. That does not remove the circumstances, how they were harmed or wronged and their inability to overcome that, that brought about a person getting to that place. The God I serve is a God of love. It is His essence and what He is known for. Biblical passages like John 3:16-17 tell us that beyond any reasonable doubt. I am comfortable knowing that if I, a flawed and frail human can grasp why such a person in deep despair would take such drastic action, will not God understand that 100 times more than I? Now, notice I earlier stated that suicide should be on a *"case by case"* basis. I say that because I believe there are blatant acts of suicide that were done with obvious premeditation, and in those cases my thought is that those persons will indeed be forfeiting eternal life in Christ. When there are circumstances like in the case of Wendy, who left no note and whose parents as you have read were overwhelmed, was it not God who obviously drew me to Bill and Sharon, for the purpose of bringing *"beauty where there were ashes?"* These *"God- incidences"* are no coincidences, this

is how God works in these cases, and this is what separates them from those blatant cases. That is a big part of the reason why I chose to believe that suicide can only be judged on such a basis as I mentioned, taking each case one at a time. Another favorite saying of mine is, *"not everyone who is 5'11 wears a size 12"*. It's not a *"one size fits all"* scenario friends, not by any means. Does the enemy push them over the edge? Yes, does he play a big part in this? Absolutely, but God sees and knows the entire circumstance. In fact, around the time of this writing, a very prominent Calvary Chapel Pastor, Jarrid Wilson, a Pastor who struggled for years with depression and who strongly advocated for mental health awareness within the local Church, who was also the founder of *"Anthem of Hope"*, after doing a funeral for a woman who took her life, then took his own life, and just hours before he did, he tweeted this;

"Loving Jesus doesn't always cure suicidal thoughts.

Loving Jesus doesn't always cure depression.

Loving Jesus doesn't always cure PTSD.

Loving Jesus doesn't always cure anxiety.

But that doesn't mean Jesus doesn't offer us companionship and comfort.

He ALWAYS does that"

Upon his death, both his Pastor, well known Evangelist Greg Laurie as well as Jarrid's wife, Juli, the mother of his 2 young children both spoke openly of *"seeing him again in heaven"*.

I'll leave you with this true story before Sharon brings you her thoughts.

This true story is about a Christian man who took his life. The experience lends an interesting perspective on the issue of Christians and suicide. The man who had killed himself was the son of a church staff member. In the short time he had been a believer, he touched many lives for Jesus Christ. His funeral was one of the most moving memorials ever attended. With more than 500 mourners gathered, for nearly two hours, person after person testified how this man had been used by God. He had pointed countless lives to faith in Christ and had shown them the way to the Father's love. Mourners left the service convinced that what had driven him to commit suicide had been his inability to shake his addiction to drugs and the failure he felt as a husband, father, and son. Although it was a sad and tragic ending, nevertheless, his life testified undeniably of Christ's redemptive power in an amazing way. **It is very difficult to believe this man went to hell.** In 1st Corinthians chapter 5, Paul made an incredible stamen about a man who was deeply involved in a sinful relationship. Paul *"let us inside"* if you will on how it is that a person can be involved in something immoral and yet still has a chance for salvation. 1 Corinthians 5:5: (CSBBible) *hand that one over to Satan for the destruction of the flesh, so that his spirit may be saved in the day of the Lord.* Did Paul actually say *"that his soul might be saved?"* Friends, do not be so quick to judge, it shows that no one can truly understand the depth of someone else's suffering or the reasons that could drive a soul to such desperation. **Only God** knows what is in a person's heart. *(Psalm 139:1-2)* Only He knows the extent of pain which might drive a person to the point of suicide.

For the record, let me share eight names of people who were close to ending their lives when the storm was brewing inside of them. I'm sure you will recognize quite a few of them and I'll let you be the judge whether they went on to make something of their lives, regardless of whether you like them or not.

Micky Dolenz
Ken Griffey Jr.
Princess Diana
Billy Joel
Elton John
Johnny Cash
Oprah Winfrey
Martin Luther King Jr.

In conclusion, it bears repeating that suicide is a terrible tragedy, but it **does not negate** the Lord's act of redemption. Our salvation rests securely in the finished work of Jesus Christ on the cross. So then, *"Everyone who calls on the name of the Lord will be saved." (Romans 10:13)* I've often wondered if Wendy's last words before she pulled the trigger might have been *"God, forgive me"*, *that's something we will never know this side of heaven, but it is certainly something very possible.*

(A Few Words from Sharon) I will begin here by addressing the last sentence in Pastor Al's thoughts, *"I've often wondered if Wendy's last words before she pulled the trigger might have been "God, forgive me"………* Bill and I both wondered this and I still do. I honestly choose to feel

that was indeed the case and one day I will see her again in Heaven. Suicide has been construed as a crime in my humble opinion, by the actual stating of the death – **_Committed_** Suicide. Committed suggests a crime. I choose to state that Wendy **died** by suicide and I am not ashamed to put it out there to folks that do not know me. If they choose to look away or not address this fact, then that is their choice. Our daughter lived for 19 years, not just only an epithet of one day. In fact, for many years, the Catholic Church forbid proper Christian burial for individuals who died by suicide. In an article from Catholic.com entitled *"What Does the Church teach about Suicide",* we read, *"Yes, for many centuries the Church taught that those who took their own lives could not be given a Christian funeral or buried in consecrated ground. Nonetheless, in so doing the Church wasn't passing judgment on the salvation of the individual soul; rather, the deprivation of Christian funeral rites was a pastoral discipline intended to teach Catholics the gravity of suicide. Although the Church no longer requires that Christian funeral rites be denied to people who die by suicide, the Church does still recognize the objective gravity of the act:*

Suicide contradicts the natural inclination of the human being to preserve and perpetuate his life. It is gravely contrary to the just love of self (CCC 2281)." Thankfully the Catholic Church today recognizes some of the factors Pastor Al spoke about earlier in this chapter when it states the following:

"Mortal sin requires full knowledge and complete consent. It presupposes knowledge of the sinful character of the

act, of its opposition to God's law. It also implies consent sufficiently deliberate to be a personal choice (CCC 1859).

When a person dies by suicide as a result of psychological impairment, such as that caused by clinical depression, the Church recognizes that he may not have been fully capable of the knowledge and consent necessary to commit mortal sin:

Grave psychological disturbances, anguish, or grave fear of hardship, suffering, or torture can diminish the responsibility of the one who has died via suicide (CCC 2282).

Far from condemning souls to hell for suicide, then, the Church teaches that salvation is possible for those who perform this act and cautions survivors against despair for their deceased loved ones."

Some of this still exists today, for instance people will often say something along these lines; *"There obviously must have been some dark, terrible secret within said family, when the truth is sometimes no one knows, including the family".*

Suicide, in most instances, is a cry for help that goes unanswered because of completed suicide being the absolute final end. There is so much we can do as a society to help people in a depressed, dark state. The first step is to really listen, to pay attention, and be observant when noticeable changes are happening within a person. Suicide survivors go through lots of years of self-infliction of the loss of their loved one, feeling that they could have or should have seen or helped to change the fateful path they were headed. That is futile in its retrospect as we can't know what goes on inside anyone, even our closest family members and friends. As I said, we can only try to be observant while also making ourselves available, if and when called upon to listen or to act as needed. As a suicide survivor, there were several books that helped me to survive the worst loss of my life. I'd like to recommend the following books that were are great help to me during those first few years and I pray they can likewise be a help to you as well:

The Bereaved Parent; by Harriet Sarnoff Schiff

Roses in December; by Marilyn Willett Heavilyn

18 No Time to Waste; by Margaret Johnson

My Son....My Son....; by Iris Bolton

After the Death of a Child; by Ann K. Finkbeiner

When the Bough Breaks; by Judith R. Bernstein, Ph.D.

There are several others, but over time I have given away many of the books that I had read to others that needed them. I did not make it a priority that I get them returned and simply asked if they could pass them on as needed to others who found themselves sadly in a similar circumstance.

Chapter Thirteen
about the Authors *(Why I Agreed To Tell My Story)*

Sharon Throop

Sharon was born in Cleveland, Ohio and at the age of 8 years old her family moved to Willowick, Ohio where they resided until she graduated high school at Eastlake North High School.

She married her high school sweetheart at the age of 19 and they had two children, a son Dale and a daughter

Wendy. Sadly the marriage did not survive and after 15 years ended in divorce. Sharon returned to the work force and it was there after a year or so that she met the love of her life, Bill Throop. After dating for a while and assuring that the blended family would not be an issue, they married in December of 1986.

Bill loved Wendy as his own and raised her with good solid values and helped her in all the ways he was able to. Sharon and Bill raised Wendy to graduate with honors and to attend college at Ohio Wesleyan University. The loss of Wendy was overbearing and when most couples do not survive the loss of a child, Bill made sure to hold Sharon up and for her to reach out to others with the deep, dark pain that only losing a child can bring.

The sad truth is that after Wendy's loss, God was the furthest thing from Sharon's world and she truly lived in an isolated cocoon for a lot of months. She did seek help from a doctor and took medication for a few months that helped her to function on somewhat of an even keel. But the truth is that it was Pastor Al who helped both Bill and Sharon find the true path of walking with our Lord Jesus Christ again.

Unfortunately Bill contracted cancer and was undergoing treatment when he suddenly passed away April of 2018. Sharon still resides in the same farmhouse and attempts to maintain the household and do what she can when she can. Although Bill's loss left its sting, this loss has been easier for her to bear, as this time she has God firmly within her soul; unlike when Wendy died and it took so long to return to Jesus again. That being said, the loss of her soulmate still hurts and having lived with Bill for over 30+ years it can be understood why. She truly misses her soulmate, best friend and husband and is only glad that he is no longer in pain or struggling with physical issues that hampered the last year of his life. Some days it comes easily, others not so much.

Sharon has joined many Bible studies at her church which provides her an outlet of learning more of God's word that can be translated to helping anyone even in this day and age. And despite all this time of loss and having recently *(last year)* lost her husband she's enlisted the aid of an organization called Griefshare, *(you can look this organization up on the internet and find a Griefshare session near you)* it is a bible based group that has 15 week sessions which include videos and discussions. They have been a good source of strength for her to remind her that she is not alone in this struggle once again of loss.

On a personal note.........How many of you have turned not only from God, but from people? As I mentioned earlier, I know I did and in the people department still do at times, but since letting the Lord into my heart and life, He has truly comforted me. And what a comfort He is! I know in my heart of hearts that He is comforting Wendy and Bill and one day we will all be together again. And please if you ever feel the need to contact me, know that I will answer you to the best of my abilities with my past/present knowledge to help you in whatever way or council you may seek. It is what Wendy and Bill would have done; I can honestly tell you that!

Why I agreed to tell my story.

The truth be told, Pastor Al came to me many years ago wanting me to tell this story, but it was only earlier this year *(2019)* that I finally told him yes and here is why friends.

Some of the reasons that I have finally agreed to put into words my loss and then finding of God's love and my faith was simply to help others. I have led a lonely life these past 18 months and have tried to better myself and allow this life to speak to others. So many have helped me these past 18 months, which has allowed me to see that I am truly never alone. It finally got into my thick headed skull that I was actually **never** alone; I always had God with me whether I thought so or not. With this in mind; in our last Griefshare session one of the group shared that she had not been close to God for a long time, but now she strives to begin her day asking Him to provide her strength and to begin her day anew. She told us that she actually thought at first it was a bunch of hooey, but now after 14 sessions she once again can look forward to her days and focuses on God more and more. She no longer worries about what the rest of her family needs to do and focuses on her relationship with God. He only wants the best for us and sometimes we blame rather than trust in the Lord.

Bill used to tell me if everyone has a talent given by God what was his? I told him that it could be something as simple as making sure that I survived and continued on my path. But, since his death I have come to understand that Bill was a very kind soul with a great sense of humor. I have come across many people since the loss of Bill and they have confirmed these same things to me. How he helped many *"behind the scenes"* and things of that nature, many I didn't even know! I was blessed to have him for so long, but we are never satisfied and I could have used some more time! However, I know he is with the Wendy-kid and that one day, I will see them both again as our wonderful Savior, Jesus has promised. Pastor Al brought the Lord back into our lives, but no one embraced our Lord as much as Bill had in his lifetime. He used to call Pastor Al, his own personal apostle.

Bill in 2011

When Bill passed away so many folks reached out to share and to help prop me up as needed. One of my old high school friends sent me a framed picture *(the one above)* with the following prose;

"He's the whisper of the leaves as you walk down the street, your husband lives on with the sound of your laughter, he's the gentle touch on your brown when you're not feeling well. He's crystallized in ever teardrop...He's the thousand winds that blow. He's the diamonds that glistens on the snow; He's the swift uplifting rush of butterflies in

107

joyous flight... He's the soft stars that shine so brightly at night. He's the map you follow with every step you take. He's your true love and nothing on earth can every separate. Not time.... Not space.... Not even death....Nothing will separate you from your Husband....You carry him inside your heart....Your loving memories live forever, and he's always with you and will never depart".
Author Unknown

As for my talent, well I have tried to be faithful to my path that seems to have been laid out for me by the Almighty Himself. I do not have much of a legacy to show for my life and little family left. It would do me a great service if anyone that needs me to help them, just simply reach out to me at the information provided below. I'm always glad to help and share whenever possible. That is what I have been all about for over 20 years and will try to honor that for as long as I am able! My current email is; sharwen48@yahoo.com *(just a keystroke away and I care!)* Blessings to you all that bought and read this book of my journey through the hardest time of my life.

Bill and Sharon in 2016

Dear friends, I leave you with the following verse that has become a sort of *"mantra"* for my life since Wendy's passing. My prayer is that it will mean to you what it has meant to me. *Philippians 4:13: I am able to do all things through Him who strengthens me.*

A Service of Memorial and Celebration
for the Precious Life of

WENDY L. SUNDERLIN
June 18, 1977 - November 12, 1996

+ + +

ONE, TAKEN TO HEART...for Wendy

A book,
so much a part of our lives,
seems lost.
Fallen,
somewhere,
out of place.
We drag about the house
in heavy shoes,
examining the empty rooms.
We open the blinds,
wash our eyes
and search the shelf for answers.
Thinking,
what could we have done
with that book,
where did we see it last?
Could a book just
wander off
like that?
Questions to throw at the moon,
while standing,
rooted in the shadows,
remembering the story.

The story.
Remember the time?
*   the page?*
*   the chapter?*
Remember?
Remember the smile?
A book can get lost,
disappear,
or simply fall to pieces,
but a story plays forever
once we've taken it to heart.

And for the rest
of what each of us will know
of eternity,
even when, barehanded,
we drag about the house
in heavy shoes,
wash our eyes
and search the shelf for answers,
the story will survive
to coax us from the empty room,
back into the moonlight,
a sister,
teaching us to dance.

- Sara Holbrook
November 15, 1996

Rev. Al Stewart, D.D.

Currently makes his home in Forest, VA. with his wife Dawn. He has 2 sons as well as a stepson. Al has pastored for over 25+ years and is currently the Pastor of Greater Grace Chapel in Lynchburg, VA. *(greatergracechapel.com)* He is a native of Waterbury, Ct. and attended Golden State School of Theology and Schofield Seminary later earning an Honorary Doctorate from Adonai International Christian University [A.I.C.U.] for his Apologetics work among Jehovah's Witnesses and Latter Day Saints. Pastor Al is also an ordained Police/Fire Chaplain through Shield of Faith Ministries and is ordained through Adonai International Fellowship Alliance [A.I.F.A.] and serves as Chaplain of Post 16, American Legion of Lynchburg, Va.

He served in the U.S. Army from 1977-80 in West Germany. He has appeared on TBN's *"Praise the Lord"* program as well as the Pondering and Midwest

Outreach Podcasts and is available on occasion to speak. He can be reached at:

PoBoy Publishing
PO Box 622
Forest, Va. 24551 *(email: rev.stuw@yahoo.com)*

Endorsements

Pastor Al's heart is obviously enormous as he has cared for this grieving family for many years. Both His & Sharon's Biblically balanced view of suicide and the need for hope in the aftermath of such a loss is frankly, a breath of fresh air. Too often, Christian leaders have jumped to an "easy and harsh" conclusion regarding the state of someone who has taken their own life. Grace and God's ability to see suicide as He does any other sin needs to be understood and preached.

- *Pastor Joel L. Rissinger, Author, Executive Pastor, Lifeway Church, President, Corporate Chaplaincy Services & The Rissinger Resource Group, LLC*

Wendy's story is a powerful story of redemption and love that can come from tragedy. Sharon relays the hurt and despair eloquently and honestly. She addresses the struggle and ache of loss, and the isolation. Al pairs that with his discussion of the stigma of losing a child to suicide. This is a book for anyone who is struggling with the loss of a loved one to suicide. It is also for those who may be struggling with suicidal ideations. As a counselor, it is refreshing to have a pastor actively address the need of people to understand that mental health is just as important as physical health, and is often tied together. His recognition of the spiritual side of suicide and the aftermath is a blessing as well.

- *Theresa Prewitt,*
  MAMFT,
  Liberty University

Suicide, the word alone makes us uncomfortable as our hearts begin to grow heavy. It is a subject that no one likes talking about, and so most people avoid addressing it at all. I understand. As a pastor, I have seen families within our church and in our community, who have been devastated by a loved one taking his or her own life. That is why I was eager to read this book by Reverend Al Stewart and Sharon Throop. I walked away hurting for Wendy's family and friends, but I also had a renewed hope, Why? Because I know God will use this story to bring "beauty from ashes". Families who have been directly impacted will find some salve for their souls. As great as that is, I truly believe the greater impact will be that someone will say no to suicide after having read this book. That is priceless. Without a doubt, this book is a **must read** *AND a* **must share.** *Thank you, Sharon Throop, for choosing to go through more hurting so others may find healing, and thank you, Reverend Al Stewart, for being a faithful servant, allowing God to use you to bring "beauty from ashes" (Isaiah 61:3).*

- *Pastor Dwight H. Weaver, Jr.,*
  Langhorne Chapel Community Church
  Evington, Virginia

This book does an excellent job explaining how each person individually grieves and gives the reader an inside voice of a parent suffering the loss of her child. When a person loses a loved one, they go through different stages of grief and those stages look different for everyone. As someone who has dealt with grief and counseled others through the grieving process, there is no time limit on the grieving process - it may take years or even a lifetime to heal. I agree with Sharon as she explains that when a person is gone, they're never gone from our hearts. With grief, there is often a struggle to find a new normal. I agree with Sharon as she wrote: "I can go out amongst the population and they may never know what lies inside the depths of my soul." In this world, there are so many times when we are walking around not knowing the suffering that is right in front of us. Furthermore, in this book, Sharon discovers God's love and the beauty of God's work in many different ways. Like many of us, she was able to find God's love through divine interventions like: bumping into someone in a store, meeting a waitress with the same name as her late daughter, Wendy, and even through helping other people that struggle with thoughts of suicide.

Sharon's coauthor of this book, Reverend Al Stewart, explains that suicidal thoughts are like a cancerous disease of the mind. In fact, as a therapist, studies have shown that 95% of people that die by suicide have a mental health issue. However, Reverend Stewart says God granted us free will and the ability to choose life through the healing power of Jesus Christ. Through the devastation, Sharon chooses to *let the Lord Jesus Christ have control of her life and it's at this time she begins to find peace. Through the pain of grief, Sharon truly finds the Beauty out of Ashes.*

- *Caryn M. Pack, BA, MHR*
Bachelor's degree in Psychology,
Oklahoma State University
Masters of Human Relations,
University of Oklahoma

Additional Books Available on Amazon Worldwide by Rev. Al Stewart via PoBoy Publishing:

"Works Revisited"
(Amazon/KDP)

"The Watchtower Revisited, Dangerous Doctrines of Jehovah's Witnesses"
(Amazon/KDP)

"Mormonism Revisited"
(Amazon/KDP)

"The Importance of Just One Revisited"
(Amazon/KDP)

"Hand's Up, Arrested by God; The Story of Ret.
Police Office & Chaplain, Bob Faubel"
(Amazon/KDP)

"How to Communicate Jesus Effectively "
(Amazon/KDP)

"East Germany Revisited, Utopia Failed"
(Amazon/KDP)

"Wesleyan/Arminian Theology Revisited"
(Amazon/KDP)

"Divine Appointments"
(Amazon/KDP)

LEAVE A REVIEW!

Choosing to be a self-publisher, I can't tell you how important leaving a good review is!

Simply type in the book title on Amazon to find the books page and click on leave a review, it's that's simple and thank you in advance! - Pastor Al

Made in the USA
Columbia, SC
04 March 2022